Gender in
International
Relations

New Directions in World Politics
John Gerard Ruggie and Helen Milner, General Editors

New Directions in World Politics
John Gerard Ruggie and Helen Milner, General Editors

Gender in International Relations

Feminist Perspectives

on Achieving

Global Security

J. Ann Tickner

Columbia University Press

New York

COLUMBIA UNIVERSITY PRESS

NEW YORK   OXFORD

Copyright © 1992 Columbia University Press

Library of Congress Cataloging-in-Publication Data

Tickner, J. Ann.
Gender in international relations : feminist perspectives on
achieving global security / J. Ann Tickner.
p.   cm.—(New directions in world politics)
Includes bibliographical references and index.
ISBN 0–231–07538–3.—ISBN 0–231–07539–1 (pbk.)
1. International relations.   2. Security, International.
3. Feminist theory.   4. Feminism.   I. Title.
JX1391.T53   1992
327.1'7—dc20   92–11103
                                                                        CIP

Casebound editions of
Columbia University Press books
are Smyth-sewn and printed
on permanent and durable
acid-free paper.

Designed by Teresa Bonner
Printed in the United States of America

c 10 9 8 7 6 5 4 3 2 1
p 10 9 8 7 6 5 4 3 2 1

To Joan, Heather, and Wendy
—feminists for the future

Contents

vii

Preface

As a scholar and teacher of international relations, I have frequently asked myself the following questions: Why are there so few women in my discipline? If I teach the field as it is conventionally defined, why are there so few readings by women to assign to my students? Why is the subject matter of my discipline so distant from women's lived experiences? Why have women been conspicuous only by their absence in the worlds of diplomacy and military and foreign policy-making?

I began to think about writing this book as an attempt to answer these questions. Having spent my childhood in London during World War II and my adolescence in New York as part of a United Nations' family, international affairs were an important part of my early life. But, as one of only three female graduate students in my year in Yale University's International Relations Program in the early 1960s, I began to notice that the academic discipline that I had chosen, in part because of these formative experiences, was not one that attracted many women. Admittedly, when I returned to graduate studies in the 1970s, the number of women entering the field had grown: while I felt less isolated, I observed that women scholars and teachers of international relations were clustered in areas such as international political economy, development studies, and international political theory. I still wondered why so few women chose national and international security studies, the privileged core of the field.

My own research has been in areas such as Third World development, North-South relations, and peace studies— areas that were far from the mainstream of international politics in the early 1980s when I began my academic career. Like many women in international relations, I did not choose to specialize in security-linked war and peace studies, usually associated with great power relations and power politics, areas central to the subject matter of the classical discipline.

As a teacher of international relations, however, I have, of necessity, familiarized myself with what some in my field would call the "important" issues of war and peace, generally defined as national security studies. But, as only one of three women out of a total of about sixty students who participated in a course on nuclear strategy at M.I.T. in the early 1980s, my contention that this is an area of international relations not heavily populated by women was strongly reinforced. Trying to familiarize myself with the arcane and esoteric language of nuclear strategy, I remembered with some sympathy how, as an undergraduate history major, I had avoided details of war-fighting strategies and weapons development.

Since I began teaching these issues myself, often using the same language that I found so alienating in my own education, I have found that, while many of my male students

seem quite comfortable with the discourse of war and weap-
onry in my introductory course on international relations, a
semester has never passed without some of my female students expressing privately that they fear they will not do
well in this course because it does not seem to be "their
subject." In trying to reassure these women that they can be
successful, I have often paused to reflect on whether this is
"my subject." Frequently, I have been the only woman on
professional panels in my field, and I am disappointed that I
cannot find more women theorists of international relations
to assign to my students. Just as the traditional subject matter of my discipline has been constructed without reference
to most of women's lived experiences, women have rarely
been portrayed as actors on the stage of international politics.

Rather than discussing strategies for bringing more women
into the international relations discipline as it is conventionally defined, I shall seek answers to my questions by bringing to light what I believe to be the masculinist underpinnings of the field. I shall also examine what the discipline
might look like if the central realities of women's day-to-day
lives were included in its subject matter. Making women's
experiences visible allows us to see how gender relations
have contributed to the way in which the field of international relations is conventionally constructed and to reexam-
ine the traditional boundaries of the field. Drawing attention
to gender hierarchies that privilege men's knowledge and
men's experiences permits us to see that it is these experiences that have formed the basis of most of our knowledge
about international politics. It is doubtful whether we can
achieve a more peaceful and just world, a goal of many
scholars both women and men who write about international
politics, while these gender hierarchies remain in place.

Although this book is an attempt to make the discipline of
international relations more relevant to women's lives, I am
not writing it only for women; I hope that its audience will
include both women and men who are seeking a more inclu-

sive approach to the way we think about international politics. Women have spoken and written on the margins of international relations because it is to the margins that their experiences have been relegated. Not until international politics is an arena that values the lived experiences of us all can we truly envisage a more comprehensive and egalitarian approach that, it is to be hoped, could lead to a more peaceful world. Because gender hierarchies have contributed to the perpetuation of global insecurities, all those concerned with international affairs—men and women alike—should also be concerned with understanding and overcoming their effects.

I have attempted to present the material in this book in a way that is accessible to readers in both the discipline of international relations and the discipline of feminist studies. Since I focus on the issue of global security, the book should also be of interest to those in the peace studies field, as well as to a more general audience seeking new ways to think about international politics. Trained in the discipline of international relations, I began my own intellectual journey toward the feminist perspectives on international relations I am presenting when I read Evelyn Fox Keller's *Reflections on Gender and Science*. When I subsequently sat in on her course on gender and science at M.I.T. in 1986, my initial thought that her feminist critique of the natural sciences could be applied to theories of international relations was confirmed.

In June 1988 I was invited to participate in one of the first conferences on gender and international relations held at the London School of Economics. In the spring of 1989 I was privileged to be able to participate in the first graduate seminar on women and international relations in the Department of International Relations at the L.S.E. During that time, my early thoughts on the subject benefited from discussions with Fred Halliday, Kathleen Newland, and Rebecca Grant. With the support of a Batchelor Ford Faculty Fellowship from Holy Cross College, I spent the remainder of that semester at the Center for Women Scholars and Research on Women at Uppsala University. I am grateful to Mona Eliasson, the director of the center, who provided support and encouragement during those early stages of this work. Readers will recognize the influence of Scandinavian peace research in my multidimensional definition of global security. Time spent at the Department of Peace and Conflict Research at Uppsala University was important in helping me to think about how I could reconceptualize this definition of global security using a feminist perspective. I am grateful to Peter Wallensteen and other members of that department for their support and interest.

On this side of the Atlantic, I am grateful to the women associated with the newly formed Feminist Theory and Gender Studies section of the International Studies Association. Through participation on panels at various I.S.A. meetings, as well as informal discussions with these women, many of my earlier ideas on gender in international relations have been sharpened or revised. For their reading and comments on particular portions of the book, I would like to thank Nazli Choucri, Irene Diamond, Jean Elshtain, Cynthia Enloe, Peter Haas, Welling Hall, Craig Murphy, Susan Okin, Carole Pateman, Spike Peterson, Anne Runyan, and Jutta Weldes. At Holy Cross College, I have appreciated the advice of my colleagues Hilde Hein, Diane Bell, and the late Maurizio Vannicelli, whose support of and insightful comments on all my work will be greatly missed in the future.

The final draft of this book was written during the academic year 1990–91 when I was a visiting research scholar at the Wellesley College Center for Research on Women. I am grateful to Susan Bailey and Jan Putnam as well as to other visiting scholars and members of the staff at the center for providing the friendly and supportive atmosphere needed to finish this project. To Peggy McIntosh I owe a particular debt of gratitude for her willingness to share many insights that have helped me to become a better feminist. I am also grateful to Holy Cross College for providing the luxury of a sabbatical leave during which this project was completed.

I should especially like to thank Robert Keohane whose initial encouragement and continued support were important to me in deciding to undertake research in what is still a very new and relatively uncharted approach to international relations. I also appreciated his thoughtful comments on this manuscript. I am grateful to Kate Wittenberg, editor in chief at Columbia University Press, who has contributed a great deal to the realization of this project from the start, and to Anne McCoy, managing editor at the press. Helen Milner, coeditor of the press's series on New Directions in World Politics, James Der Derian, and Mona Harrington offered thoughtful and useful suggestions on the manuscript. Finally, to my husband, Hayward Alker, I owe a special word of appreciation. While he has always been a source of support for my professional endeavors, I have also benefited enormously from his comments on the entire manuscript.

Gender in
International
Relations

1

Engendered Insecurities: Feminist Perspectives on International Relations

Too often the great decisions are originated and given form in bodies made up wholly of men, or so completely dominated by them that whatever of special value women have to offer is shunted aside without expression.
—ELEANOR ROOSEVELT

Representation of the world, like the world itself, is the work of men; they describe it from their own point of view, which they confuse with absolute truth.
—SIMONE DE BEAUVOIR

As Eleanor Roosevelt and countless others have observed, international politics is a man's world. It is a world inhabited by diplomats, soldiers, and international civil servants most of whom are men. Apart from the occasional head of state, there is little evidence to suggest that women have played much of a role in shaping foreign policy in any country in the twentieth century. In the United States in 1987, women constituted less than 5 percent of the senior Foreign Service ranks, and in the same year, less than 4 percent of the executive positions in the Department of Defense were held by women.[1] Although it is true that women are underrepresented in all top-level government positions in the United States and else-

1

where, they encounter additional difficulties in positions having to do with international politics. The following stories can help us to understand why.

Before the superpower summit in Geneva in 1985, Donald Regan, then White House chief of staff, told a *Washington Post* reporter that women would not understand the issues at stake at that meeting. As reported in the *Boston Globe* of October 10, 1985, Regan claimed that women are "not . . . going to understand [missile] throw-weights or what is happening in Afghanistan or what is happening in human rights.. . . . Some women will, but most women . . . would rather read the human interest stuff of what happened." Protesting Regan's remarks, feminists cited women's prominent roles in the various peace movements of the twentieth century as evidence of their competency in international affairs.[2]

When Bella Abzug entered the House of Representatives in 1972, she claimed that ending the war in Vietnam was the most important item on the congressional agenda and the one on which she most wanted to work as the representative of the many women and men in her district who opposed the war. With this goal in mind, Abzug requested a seat on the House Armed Services Committee, a committee on which, in 1972, no woman had served in the past twenty-two years. Abzug's request was denied by members of the House leadership, one of whom suggested that the Agriculture Committee would be more appropriate. In her account of this incident, Abzug notes that, of the twelve women in the House of Representatives in 1972, five were assigned to the Education and Labor Committee, evidence that suggests that women in politics are channeled into certain arenas of public policy that are perceived as "women's issues."[3]

More recently, a picture of Congresswoman Patricia Schroeder crying on her husband's shoulder, which appeared on the front page of several major American newspapers after she withdrew from the presidential primary campaign in September 1987, stimulated subsequent discussion about her suitability as a presidential candidate. The discussion revealed that, even though Schroeder is one of the very few women who has served on the House Armed Services Committee, many people in the United States had strong misgivings over the thought of an emotional woman with her finger on the nuclear button.[4]

Each of these stories reinforces the belief, widely held in the United States and throughout the world by both men and women, that military and foreign policy are arenas of policy-making least appropriate for women. Strength, power, autonomy, independence, and rationality, all typically associated with men and masculinity, are characteristics we most value in those to whom we entrust the conduct of our foreign policy and the defense of our national interest. Those women in the peace movements, whom feminist critics of Donald Regan cited as evidence for women's involvement in international affairs, are frequently branded as naive, weak, and even unpatriotic. When we think about the definition of a patriot, we generally think of a man, often a soldier who defends his homeland, most especially his women and children, from dangerous outsiders. (We sometimes even think of a missile or a football team.) The Schroeder story suggests that even women who have experience in foreign policy issues are perceived as being too emotional and too weak for the tough life-and-death decisions required for the nation's defense. Weakness is always considered a danger when issues of national security are at stake: the president's dual role as commander in chief reinforces our belief that qualities we associate with "manliness" are of utmost importance in the selection of our presidents.

The few women who do make it into the foreign policy establishment often suffer from this negative perception: Jeane Kirkpatrick is one such example. Attracted by her authoritative and forceful public style and strong anticommunist rhetoric, Ronald Reagan appointed Kirkpatrick as ambassador to the United Nations in 1981. Yet in spite of the visibility she achieved due to her strong stance against anti-American voices at the United Nations, Kirkpatrick complained of not being taken seriously by her peers both in the United Nations and in the U.S. foreign policy establishment. Although other American ambassadors to the United Nations have also complained that they lack influence over U.S. foreign policy-making, Kirkpatrick specifically attributed this lack of respect to her sex: describing herself to one reporter as a "mouse in a man's world," Kirkpatrick claimed that her views were seldom listened to and that she failed to have any effect whatsoever on the course of American foreign policy.[5]

The experiences of Abzug, Schroeder, and Kirkpatrick—women with very different political perspectives (two liberal Democrats and one conservative Republican)—are examples of the difficulties that women face when they try to enter the elite world of foreign policy decision-making. In this book, however, I do not intend to focus on strategies to increase the number of women in high foreign policy positions. I believe that these gender-related difficulties are symptomatic of a much deeper issue that I do wish to address: the extent to which international politics is such a thoroughly masculinized sphere of activity that women's voices are considered inauthentic. Therefore my attempt is to step back from the experiences of the few women who have tried to operate in the world of international politics, sometimes even successfully, and to examine how this world is constructed. By analyzing some of the writings of those who have tried to describe, explain, and prescribe for the behavior of states in the international system, we can begin to understand some of the deeper reasons for women's pervasive exclusion from foreign policy-making—for it is in the way that we are taught to think about international politics that the attitudes I have described are shaped.

With its focus on the "high" politics of war and Realpolitik, the traditional Western academic discipline of international relations privileges issues that grow out of men's experiences; we are socialized into believing that war and power politics are spheres of activity with which men have a special affinity and that their voices in describing and prescribing for this world are therefore likely to be more authentic. The roles traditionally ascribed to women—in reproduction, in households, and even in the economy—are generally considered irrelevant to the traditional construction of the field. Ignoring women's experiences contributes not only to their exclusion but also to a process of self-selection that results in an overwhelmingly male population both in the foreign policy world and in the academic field of international relations. This selection process begins with the way we are taught to think about world politics; if women's experiences were to be included, a radical redefinition of the field would have to take place.

The purpose of this book is to begin to think about how the discipline of international relations might look if gender were included as a category of analysis and if women's experiences were part of the subject matter out of which its theories are constructed. Until gender hierarchies are eliminated, hierarchies that privilege male characteristics and men's knowledge and experiences, and sustain the kind of attitudes toward women in foreign policy that I have described, I do not believe that the marginalization of women in matters related to international politics is likely to change.

Gender in International Relations

While the purpose of this book is to introduce gender as a category of analysis into the discipline of international relations, the marginalization of women in the arena of foreign policy-making through the kind of gender stereotyping that I have described suggests that international politics has always been a gendered activity in the modern state system. Since foreign and military policy-making has been largely conducted by men, the discipline that analyzes these activities is bound to be primarily about men and masculinity. We seldom realize we think in these terms, however; in most fields of knowledge we have become accustomed to equating what is human with what is masculine. Nowhere is this

5

more true than in international relations, a discipline that, while it has for the most part resisted the introduction of gender into its discourse, bases its assumptions and explanations almost entirely on the activities and experiences of men. Any attempt to introduce a more explicitly gendered analysis into the field must therefore begin with a discussion of masculinity.

Masculinity and politics have a long and close association. Characteristics associated with "manliness," such as toughness, courage, power, independence, and even physical strength, have, throughout history, been those most valued in the conduct of politics, particularly international politics. Frequently, manliness has also been associated with violence and the use of force, a type of behavior that, when conducted in the international arena, has been valorized and applauded in the name of defending one's country.

This celebration of male power, particularly the glorification of the male warrior, produces more of a gender dichotomy than exists in reality for, as R. W. Connell points out, this stereotypical image of masculinity does not fit most men. Connell suggests that what he calls "hegemonic masculinity," a type of culturally dominant masculinity that he distinguishes from other subordinated masculinities, is a socially constructed cultural ideal that, while it does not correspond to the actual personality of the majority of men, sustains patriarchal authority and legitimizes a patriarchal political and social order.[6] Hegemonic masculinity is sustained through its opposition to various subordinated and devalued masculinities, such as homosexuality, and, more important, through its relation to various devalued femininities. Socially constructed gender differences are based on socially sanctioned, unequal relationships between men and women that reinforce compliance with men's stated superiority. Nowhere in the public realm are these stereotypical gender images more apparent than in the realm of international politics, where the characteristics associated with hegemonic masculinity are projected onto the behavior of states whose success as international actors is measured in terms of their power capabilities and capacity for self-help and autonomy.

Connell's definition of hegemonic masculinity depends on its opposition to and unequal relationship with various subordinated femininities. Many contemporary feminists draw on similarly socially constructed, or engendered, relationships in their definition of gender difference. Historically, differences between men and women have usually been ascribed to biology. But when feminists use the term *gender* today, they are not generally referring to biological differences between males and females, but to a set of culturally shaped and defined characteristics associated with masculinity and femininity. These characteristics can and do vary across time and place. In this view, biology may constrain behavior, but it should not be used "deterministically" or "naturally" to justify practices, institutions, or choices that could be other than they are. While what it means to be a man or a woman varies across cultures and history, in most cultures gender differences signify relationships of inequality and the domination of women by men.

Joan Scott similarly characterizes gender as "a constitutive element of social relationships based on perceived differences between the sexes, and . . . a primary way of signifying relationships of power."[7] Indeed one could characterize most contemporary feminist scholarship in terms of the dual beliefs that gender difference has played an important and essential role in the structuring of social inequalities in much of human history and that the resulting differences in self-identifications, human understandings, social status, and power relationships are unjustified.

Scott claims that the way in which our understanding of gender signifies relationships of power is through a set of normative concepts that set forth interpretations of the meanings of symbols. In Western culture, these concepts take the form of fixed binary oppositions that categorically assert the meaning of masculine and feminine and hence legitimize a set of unequal social relationships.[8] Scott and many other contemporary feminists assert that, through our use of language, we come to perceive the world through these binary oppositions. Our Western understanding of gender is based on a set of culturally determined binary distinctions, such as public versus private, objective versus subjective, self versus other, reason versus emotion, autonomy versus relatedness, and culture versus nature; the first of each pair of characteristics is typically associated with masculinity, the second with femininity.[9] Scott claims that the hierarchical construction of these distinctions can take on a fixed and permanent quality that perpetuates women's oppression: therefore they must be challenged. To do so we must analyze the way these binary oppositions operate in different contexts and, rather than accepting them as fixed, seek to displace their hierarchical construction.[10] When many of these differences between women and men are no longer assumed to be natural or fixed, we can examine how relations of gender inequality are constructed and sustained in various arenas of public and private life. In committing itself to gender as a category of analysis, contemporary feminism also commits itself to gender equality as a social goal.

Extending Scott's challenge to the field of international relations, we can immediately detect a similar set of hierarchical binary oppositions. But in spite of the seemingly obvious association of international politics with the masculine characteristics described above, the field of international relations is one of the last of the social sciences to be touched by gender analysis and feminist perspectives.[11] The reason for this, I believe, is not that the field is gender neutral, meaning that the introduction of gender is irrelevant to its subject matter as many scholars believe, but that it is so thoroughly masculinized that the workings of these hierarchical gender relations are hidden.

Framed in its own set of binary distinctions, the discipline of international relations assumes similarly hierarchical relationships when it posits an anarchic world "outside" to be defended against through the accumulation and rational use of power. In political discourse, this becomes translated into stereotypical notions about those who inhabit the outside. Like women, foreigners are frequently portrayed as "the other": nonwhites and tropical countries are often depicted as irrational, emotional, and unstable, characteristics that are also attributed to women. The construction of this discourse and the way in which we are taught to think about international politics closely parallel the way in which we are socialized into understanding gender differences. To ignore these hierarchical constructions and their relevance to power is therefore to risk perpetuating these relationships of domination and subordination. But before beginning to describe what the field of international relations might look like if gender were included as a central category of analysis, I shall give a brief historical overview of the field as it has traditionally been constructed.

International Relations Theory in the Cold War Era

Realism

Writing on the eve of the Second World War, historian E. H. Carr claimed that it was the devastating events of World War I that motivated the founding of the discipline of international relations. Before 1914 international relations had been largely the concern of professional practitioners. But the enormous destruction caused by World War I, and the search for new methods to prevent its happening again, brought demands for the democratization of both the theory and practice of international relations.[12] According to Carr, the initial course of this new academic discipline was marked by a passionate desire to prevent another war. In the interwar period, it focused on international law and collective security, epitomized in the League of Nations, as mechanisms with which to prevent future conflicts. But when the limitations of the League and its collective security system were seen as contributing to the outbreak of World War II, the discipline turned to what its proponents have labeled political realism.

Thus the discipline of international relations began as a field that was concerned with breaking the seemingly inevitable cycle of international war. But when a war of even greater devastation broke out in 1939, the disillusionment with what was seen as mistaken idealism, embodied in pacifist policies of democratic states in the 1930s, moved certain scholars toward what they termed a more "realistic" approach to international politics. Realist scholars and practitioners such as George Kennan and Henry Kissinger, noting the dangers of popular passions and the influence of uninformed citizens on foreign policy, argued for the conduct of foreign affairs by detached "objective" elites insulated from the dangers of the moralism and legalism that had had such detrimental effects on earlier American foreign policy.[13] Realists claimed that conflict was inevitable: the best way to assure the security of states is therefore to prepare for war.

While most contemporary scholars of international relations have drawn on the historical writings of the classical Greeks as well as on those of early modern Western political theorists such as Machiavelli, Hobbes, and Rousseau, the central concern of realism, the dominant paradigm in international relations since 1945, has been with issues of war and national security in the post–World War II international system.[14] Profoundly influenced by events in Europe in the 1930s and 1940s whence many of its early scholars came, political realism has been primarily concerned with explaining the causes of international wars and the rise and fall of states. Generally Anglo-American in their orientation, realists, described by one author as the "fathers of the classical tradition,"[15] have concentrated their investigations on the power-balancing activities of the great powers.

Reacting against the failure of what they have termed the "idealist" tradition of the early twentieth century, realists take as their basic assumption a dangerous world devoid of an overarching authority to keep the peace. In this "anarchical" world, realists prescribe the accumulation of power and military strength to assure state survival, the protection of an orderly "domestic" space, and the pursuit of legitimate national interests beyond one's territorial boundaries. The state of Cold War in the latter half of the twentieth century led many of these scholars to focus on Soviet-American relations and military arms races and ensured the predominance of realist explanations of and prescriptions for state behavior in the international system.

Since many of the early writers in the classical realist tradition were European men whose lives had been disrupted by the ideologies of totalitarian regimes of the 1930s, realism strove for an objectivist methodology that, by discovering generalizable laws, could offer universalistic explanations for the behavior of states across time and space. Claiming that ideology was a cloak for the operation of Realpolitik, the goal was to be able to exercise more control over an unpredictable international environment. For realists, morality is problematic in the tough world of international politics; in fact the exercise of moral restraint, epitomized by the policies of British prime minister Neville Chamberlain in the interwar period, can be a prescription for disaster. In the United States in the 1960s, however, classical realism came under attack, not so much for its basic assumptions and goals but for its methodology, which critics faulted for failing to live up to the standards of a positivist science. These early critics of realism noted its imprecision and lack of scientific rigor. In an attempt to make the methodology of international relations more rigorous and inject a greater precision into the field, critics of classical realism advocated the collection and analysis of data relating to wars and other international transactions.[16]

Answering these critics, neorealists have attempted to develop a positivist methodology with which to build a truly objective "science" of international relations. Neorealists have used models from economics, biology, and physics, which they claim can offer universal explanations for the behavior of states in the international system.[17] The depersonalization of the discipline, which results when methodologies are borrowed from the natural sciences and statistics, has been carried to its extreme in national security studies, a subfield that has sought, through the use of operations research and game theoretic models, to analyze strategies for nuclear deterrence and nuclear war-fighting "rationally."[18]

The Challenge to Realism

The promise of constructing a grand theory of international relations proved illusory. Knowledge construction in the discipline has generally been driven by real world events, and realism appeared best to describe the political behavior of the great powers during periods of high political tension. In the early 1970s, realism was severely challenged at a time when the declining intensity of the Cold War and a dramatic rise in oil prices catapulted issues other than war and peace and Soviet-American relations to the top of the foreign policy agenda. The perceived challenge to national security, mounted by the action of the OPEC cartel, prompted some scholars to suggest that international relations must pay more attention to issues associated with economic interdependence and to activities of nonstate actors. This "interdependence" school also challenged realism's exclusive focus on political conflict and power politics in the international system by calling attention to relations between states, such as the United States and Canada or Western Europe, where war was not expected. Interdependence scholars claimed that the traditional approach was particularly unsuitable for explaining economic conflicts between advanced capitalist states.[19]

A more fundamental challenge to realism came from scholars influenced by the Marxist tradition. Motivated by a different agenda, one that emphasizes issues of equality and justice rather than issues of order and control, scholars using a variety of more radical approaches attempted to move the field away from its excessively Western focus toward a consideration of those marginalized areas of the world system that had been subject to Western colonization. When it became evident, in the 1970s, that promises of prosperity and the elimination of poverty in these newly independent states were not being fulfilled, these scholars turned their attention to the world economy, the workings of which, they believed, served to perpetuate the unevenness of development between and within states. Many of them claimed that a structural condition known as dependency locked these states on the peripheries of the world system into a detrimental relationship with the centers of political and economic power, denying them the possibility of autonomous development.[20] Marxists emphasized class divisions that exist in, and derive from, the world market and that cut across state boundaries. Peace researchers began to use the term *structural violence* to denote a condition whereby those on the margins of the international system were condemned to a shorter life expectancy through the uneven allocation of the resources of global capitalism.[21]

The introduction of competing theories and approaches and the injection of these new issues and actors into the subject matter of international relations were accompanied by a shift to a more normative approach to the field. For example, the world order perspective asked how humanity could significantly reduce the likelihood of international violence and create minimally acceptable conditions of worldwide economic well-being, social justice, ecological stability, and democratic participation in decision-making processes.[22] World order scholars questioned whether the state was an adequate instrument for solving the multiplicity of problems on the international agenda. Militarized states can be a threat to the security of their own populations; economic inequality, poverty, and constraints on resources were seen as the results of the workings of global capitalism and thus beyond the control of individual states. State boundaries cannot be protected against environmental pollution, an issue that can be addressed only by international collective action. World order scholars rejected realist claims of objectivity and positivist conceptions in the international relations discipline; adopting a specifically normative stance, they have postulated possible alternate futures that could offer the promise of equality and justice and investigated how these alternative futures could be achieved.[23]

In realism's subject matter, as well as in its quest for a scientific methodology, we can detect an orientation that corresponds to some of the masculine-linked characteristics I described above, such as the emphasis on power and autonomy and claims to objectivity and rationality. But among realism's critics, virtually no attention has been given to gender as a category of analysis. Scholars concerned with structural violence have paid little attention to how women are affected by global politics or the workings of the world economy, nor to the fact that hierarchical gender relations are interrelated with other forms of domination that they do address.[24] In developing a perspective on international relations that does address the effects of these gender hierarchies, I shall therefore be drawing on feminist theories from other disciplines to see how they can contribute to our understanding of gender in international relations.

Contemporary Feminist Theories

Just as there are multiple approaches within the discipline of international relations, there are also multiple approaches in contemporary feminist theory that come out of various disciplinary traditions and paradigms. While it is obvious that not all women are feminists, feminist theories are constructed out of the experiences of women in their many and varied circumstances, experiences that have generally been rendered invisible by most intellectual disciplines.

Most contemporary feminist perspectives define themselves in terms of reacting to traditional liberal feminism

that, since its classic formulation in the works of Mary Woll-
stonecraft and John Stuart Mill, has sought to draw attention
to and eliminate the legal restraints barring women's access
to full participation in the public world.[25] Most contemporary feminist scholars, other than liberals, claim that the
sources of discrimination against women run much deeper
than legal restraints: they are emeshed in the economic,
cultural, and social structures of society and thus do not end
when legal restraints are removed. Almost all feminist perspectives have been motivated by the common goal of attempting to describe and explain the sources of gender inequality, and hence women's oppression, and to seek strategies to end them.

Feminists claim that women are oppressed in a multiplicity of ways that depend on culture, class, and race as well as
on gender. Rosemary Tong suggests that we can categorize
various contemporary feminist theories according to the ways
in which they view the causes of women's oppression. While
Marxist feminists believe that capitalism is the source of
women's oppression, radical feminists claim that women are
oppressed by the system of patriarchy that has existed under
almost all modes of production. Patriarchy is institutional-
ized through legal and economic, as well as social and cultural institutions. Some radical feminists argue that the low
value assigned to the feminine characteristics described above
also contributes to women's oppression. Feminists in the
psychoanalytic tradition look for the source of women's
oppression deep in the psyche, in gender relationships into
which we are socialized from birth.

Socialist feminists have tried to weave these various approaches together into some kind of a comprehensive explanation of women's oppression. Socialist feminists claim that
women's position in society is determined both by structures
of production in the economy and by structures of reproduction in the household, structures that are reinforced by the
early socialization of children into gender roles. Women's
unequal status in all these structures must be eliminated for

full equality to be achieved. Socialist feminism thus tries to understand the position of women in their multiple roles in order to find a single standpoint from which to explain their condition. Using standpoint in the sense that it has been used by Marxists, these theorists claim that those who are oppressed have a better understanding of the sources of their oppression than their oppressors. "A standpoint is an engaged vision of the world opposed and superior to dominant ways of thinking."[26]

This notion of standpoint has been seriously criticized by postmodern feminists who argue that a unified representation of women across class, racial, and cultural lines is an impossibility. Just as feminists more generally have criticized existing knowledge that is grounded in the experiences of white Western males, postmodernists claim that feminists themselves are in danger of essentializing the meaning of woman when they draw exclusively on the experiences of white Western women: such an approach runs the additional risk of reproducing the same dualizing distinctions that feminists object to in patriarchal discourse.[27] Postmodernists believe that a multiplicity of women's voices must be heard lest feminism itself become one more hierarchical system of knowledge construction.

Any attempt to construct feminist perspectives on international relations must take this concern of postmodernists seriously; as described above, dominant approaches to international relations have been Western-centered and have focused their theoretical investigations on the activities of the great powers. An important goal for many feminists has been to attempt to speak for the marginalized and oppressed: much of contemporary feminism has also recognized the need to be sensitive to the multiple voices of women and the variety of circumstances out of which they speak. Developing perspectives that can shed light on gender hierarchies as they contribute to women's oppression worldwide must therefore be sensitive to the dangers of constructing a Western-centered approach. Many Western feminists are understandably apprehensive about replicating men's knowledge by generalizing from the experiences of white Western women. Yet to be unable to speak for women only further reinforces the voices of those who have constructed approaches to international relations out of the experiences of men.

"[Feminists] need a home in which everyone has a room of her own, but one in which the walls are thin enough to permit a conversation."[28] Nowhere is this more true than in these early attempts to bring feminist perspectives to bear on international politics, a realm that has been divisive in both its theory and its practice. Having presented multiparadigmatic, multiperspective descriptions of both disciplines, I shall be drawing on and synthesizing a variety of feminist perspectives as I seek to develop a gendered analysis of some of the major approaches to international relations.

Feminist Theories and International Relations

Since, as I have suggested, the world of international politics is a masculine domain, how could feminist perspectives contribute anything new to its academic discourses? Many male scholars have already noted that, given our current technologies of destruction and the high degree of economic inequality and environmental degradation that now exists, we are desperately in need of changes in the way world politics is conducted; many of them are attempting to prescribe such changes. For the most part, however, these critics have ignored the extent to which the values and assumptions that drive our contemporary international system are intrinsically related to concepts of masculinity; privileging these values constrains the options available to states and their policymakers. All knowledge is partial and is a function of the knower's lived experience in the world. Since knowledge about the behavior of states in the international system depends on assumptions that come out of men's experiences, it ignores a large body of human experience that has the potential for increasing the range of options and opening up new ways of thinking about interstate practices. Theoretical perspectives that depend on a broader range of human experience are important for women and men alike, as we seek new ways of thinking about our contemporary dilemmas.

Conventional international relations theory has concentrated on the activities of the great powers at the center of the system. Feminist theories, which speak out of the various experiences of women—who are usually on the margins of society and interstate politics—can offer us some new insights on the behavior of states and the needs of individuals, particularly those on the peripheries of the international system. Feminist perspectives, constructed out of the experiences of women, can add a new dimension to our understanding of the world economy; since women are frequently the first casualties in times of economic hardship, we might also gain some new insight into the relationship between militarism and structural violence.

However, feminist theories must go beyond injecting women's experiences into different disciplines and attempt to challenge the core concepts of the disciplines themselves. Concepts central to international relations theory and practice, such as power, sovereignty, and security, have been framed in terms that we associate with masculinity. Drawing on feminist theories to examine and critique the meaning of these and other concepts fundamental to international politics could help us to reformulate these concepts in ways that might allow us to see new possibilities for solving our current insecurities. Suggesting that the personal is political, feminist scholars have brought to our attention distinctions between public and private in the domestic polity: examining these artificial boundary distinctions in the domestic polity could shed new light on international boundaries, such as those between anarchy and order, which are so fundamental to the conceptual framework of realist discourse.

Most contemporary feminist perspectives take the gender inequalities that I have described above as a basic assumption. Feminists in various disciplines claim that feminist theories, by revealing and challenging these gender hierarchies, have the potential to transform disciplinary paradigms. By introducing gender into the discipline of international relations, I hope to challenge the way in which the field has traditionally been constructed and to examine the extent to which the practices of international politics are related to these gender inequalities. The construction of hierarchical binary oppositions has been central to theorizing about international relations.[29] Distinctions between domestic and foreign, inside and outside, order and anarchy, and center and periphery have served as important assumptions in theory construction and as organizing principles for the way we view the world. Just as realists center their explanations on the hierarchical relations between states and Marxists on unequal class relations, feminists can bring to light gender hierarchies embedded in the theories and practices of world politics and allow us to see the extent to which all these systems of domination are interrelated.

As Sarah Brown argues, a feminist theory of international relations is an act of political commitment to understanding the world from the perspective of the socially subjugated. "There is the need to identify the as yet unspecified relation between the construction of power and the construction of gender in international relations."[30] Acknowledging, as most feminist theories do, that these hierarchies are socially constructed, also allows us to envisage conditions necessary for their transcendence.

Feminist Perspectives on International Relations in the Contemporary World

The dramatic events of the late 1980s and early 1990s brought to light many of the shortcomings in realist explanations noted by critics for some time. Whereas the world wars of the first half of the twentieth century involved the transgression of great powers across international boundaries, most of the conflicts of the second half have taken place inside or across the boundaries of weak states. Although they have frequently involved at least one of the great powers, many of these conflicts have not been fought to protect international boundaries but over ethnic or religious issues, or issues of national identity and national liberation. The militarization of the South, with weapons sold or given by the North, has resulted in a situation whereby the state is often perceived, not as a protector against outside dangers, but as the ultimate threat to the security of its civilian population. The precarious armed peace that characterized the relationship between the two superpowers during the Cold War owed whatever stability it achieved not to military strength but to the threat of nuclear obliteration of winners and losers alike: nuclear weapons and other modern military technologies continue to pose the threat of mass destruction.

These new threats to security demand new solutions quite at odds with the power politics prescriptions of traditional international relations theory. As we face the prospect that, by the year 2000, 80 percent of the world's population will live in the South, we in the West can no longer afford to privilege a tradition of scholarship that focuses on the concerns and ambitions of the great powers. Faced with a stubborn gap in living standards between the rich and the poor that some observers doubt can ever be overcome, realist prescriptions of self-help are inappropriate; the health of the global economy depends on the health of all its members. Environmental degradation, a relatively new item on the agenda of international relations, threatens rich and poor alike and appears intransigent to state-centered solutions. Along with the traditional issues of war and peace, the discipline of international relations is increasingly challenged by the necessity of analyzing the realities of economic and ecological interdependence and finding ways of mitigating their negative consequences. We must also face the reality of how easily these wider security issues, which threaten the survival of the earth and all its inhabitants, disappear from the agenda when military crises escalate.

Faced with a world turned upside down, the conventional discipline of international relations has recently been undergoing a more fundamental challenge to its theoretical underpinnings. Certain scholars are now engaged in a "third debate" that questions the empirical and positivist foundations of the field.[31] Postpositivist approaches question what they claim are realism's ahistorical attempts to posit universal truths about the international system and the behavior of its member states. Like many contemporary feminists, these scholars argue that all knowledge is socially constructed and is grounded in the time, place, and social context of the investigator. Focusing on the use of language, many of these writers claim that our knowledge about the international system comes to us from accounts written by those in a position of power who use their knowledge for purposes of control and furthering their own interests.[32] These scholars assert that, while realism presents itself as an objective account of reality that claims to explain the workings of the prevailing international order, it is also an ideology that has served to legitimize and sustain that order.[33] While many of the previous challengers of realism, discussed above, still spoke in terms of large depersonalized structures—such as the international system of states or the capitalist world economy—many of these poststructuralist writers attempt to speak for disempowered individuals on the margins of the international system. Besides questioning the ability of the state or global capitalism to solve contemporary problems, they pose more fundamental questions about the construction of the state as a political space and a source of identity.

These contemporary critiques bring the international relations discourse closer to some of the feminist perspectives that I have described above: yet issues of gender have been raised only marginally. In subsequent chapters, I shall insert gender more centrally into these disciplinary debates. I shall examine some of the theoretical approaches introduced in this chapter to see to what extent their assumptions and explanations depend on historical understandings of masculinity and femininity and the experiences of men. I shall then ask how, if these gender hierarchies were made explicit and the experiences of women included, this would challenge the theoretical frameworks of these various approaches. I shall also examine what effect feminist perspectives would have on the way the field and its central concepts have been defined.

The following three chapters will focus on three topics: national security, political economy, and the natural environment. Besides being central to the contemporary agenda of international relations scholarship, these topics constitute the framework within which an important redefinition of the meaning of security is currently taking place. The achievement of security has always been central to the normative concerns of international relations scholars. But dissatisfied with the traditional models of national security, which focus exclusively on military security, certain scholars of international relations have begun to use the term *common security* to envisage a type of security that is global and multidimensional with political, economic, and ecological facets that are as important as its military dimensions. The security of individuals and their natural environment are considered as well as the security of the state. Certain peace researchers are beginning to define security in terms of the elimination of physical, structural, and ecological violence.[34] Moving the consideration of violence beyond its relation to physical violence allows us to move beyond simplistic dichotomies between war and peace to a consideration of the conditions necessary for a just peace, defined more broadly than simply the absence of war.

Defining security in terms of the elimination of physical, structural, and ecological violence is quite compatible with feminist theories that have long been concerned with all these issues.[35] Thinking of security in multidimensional terms

22

allows us to get away from prioritizing military issues, issues that have been central to the agenda of traditional international relations but that are the furthest removed from women's experiences. Many of the values promoted by supporters of common security are similar to the characteristics that, in our culture, are associated with femininity. Yet, none of this new thinking has considered security from a gendered perspective. Any feminist perspective would argue that a truly comprehensive security cannot be achieved until gender relations of domination and subordination are eliminated.

I shall begin my investigation of gendered perspectives on global security in chapter 2 with an examination of the concept of national security, the way in which security has traditionally been defined in international relations. I shall examine realism, the approach that has been primarily concerned with issues of national security. I shall analyze the extent to which realist assumptions about the international system and the states that compose it rely on the experiences of men and privilege values that we have come to associate with masculinity. If we were to include women's experiences in our assumptions about the security-seeking behavior of states, how would it change the way in which we think about national security? Given the sexual division of labor, men's association with violence has been legitimated through war and the instruments of the state. Feminist perspectives must introduce the issue of domestic violence and analyze how the boundaries between public and private, domestic and international, political and economic, are permeable and interrelated.

In chapter 3, I shall discuss the three dominant approaches to international political economy—liberalism, economic nationalism, and Marxism—and ask how the introduction of gender would affect the assumptions, explanations, and predictions of these three paradigms. Just as Marxists have argued that the workings of the world economy cannot be understood without reference to class, feminists make a similar claim with reference to gender. I shall examine the individual, the state, and class—the central units of analysis for liberalism, economic nationalism, and Marxism, respectively—to see whether these units of analysis evidence a masculinist orientation in the way they are described and in the interests they represent. I shall suggest that constructing perspectives on international political economy that include the insights of feminist theories and the economic activities of women could give us a different perspective on the workings of the world economy and the achievement of economic security for women and men alike.

In chapter 4, I shall explore some of the writings on the natural environment, the most recent issue on the agenda of the discipline of international relations. I shall trace the foundations of this newly emerging field of ecopolitics back to the nineteenth-century tradition of geopolitics. I shall argue that both this earlier tradition of geopolitics and most of the contemporary work on ecopolitics are masculine in their orientation, with common roots in an Enlightenment science whose goal was the domination of nature. Drawing on the work of ecofeminists, I shall then construct a feminist perspective on ecology that, I will argue, is more inclusive and egalitarian and that therefore offers more promise for the achievement of ecological security.

As Sarah Brown suggests, a genuinely emancipatory feminist international relations will take gender difference as its starting point but it will not take it as given. While attempting to explain how gender has been constructed and maintained in international relations, we must also see how it can be removed.[36] A world that is more secure for us all cannot be achieved until the oppressive gender hierarchies that operate to frame the way in which we think about and engage in international politics are dismantled. In my final chapter I shall argue that the feminist perspectives on international relations that I develop throughout the book are but an intermediate step toward the eventual goal of a nongendered

perspective. I shall also argue that this nongendered perspective could truly offer us a more inclusively human way
of thinking about our collective future, a future in which
women and men could share equally in the construction of a
safer and more just world.

2

Man, the State, and War: Gendered Perspectives on National Security

It is not in giving life but in risking life that man is raised above the animal: that is why superiority has been accorded in humanity not to the sex that brings forth but to that which kills.
—SIMONE DE BEAUVOIR

The man's duty, as a member of the commonwealth, is to assist in the maintenance, in the advance, in the defence of the state. The woman's duty, as a member of the commonwealth, is to assist in the ordering, in the comforting, and in the beautiful adornment of the state.
—JOHN RUSKIN

If we do not redefine manhood, war is inevitable.
—PAUL FUSSELL

In the face of what is generally perceived as a dangerous international environment, states have ranked national security high in terms of their policy priorities. According to international relations scholar Kenneth Waltz, the state conducts its affairs in the "brooding shadow of violence," and therefore war could break out at any time.[1] In the name of national security, states have justified large defense budgets, which take priority over domestic spending, military conscription of their

I owe the title of this chapter to Kenneth Waltz's book *Man, the State, and War.*

young adult male population, foreign invasions, and the curtailment of civil liberties. The security of the state is perceived as a core value that is generally supported unquestioningly by most citizens, particularly in time of war. While the role of the state in the twentieth century has expanded to include the provision of domestic social programs, national security often takes precedence over the social security of individuals.

When we think about the provision of national security we enter into what has been, and continues to be, an almost exclusively male domain. While most women support what they take to be legitimate calls for state action in the interests of international security, the task of defining, defending, and advancing the security interests of the state is a man's affair, a task that, through its association with war, has been especially valorized and rewarded in many cultures throughout history. As Simone de Beauvoir's explanation for male superiority suggests, giving one's life for one's country has been considered the highest form of patriotism, but it is an act from which women have been virtually excluded. While men have been associated with defending the state and advancing its international interests as soldiers and diplomats, women have typically been engaged in the "ordering" and "comforting" roles both in the domestic sphere, as mothers and basic needs providers, and in the caring professions, as teachers, nurses, and social workers.[2] The role of women with respect to national security has been ambiguous: defined as those whom the state and its men are protecting, women have had little control over the conditions of their protection.

I shall begin this chapter by examining the contemporary realist analysis of national security, concentrating on the work of Hans Morgenthau and Kenneth Waltz, two scholars of international relations whom I define in chapter 1 as a classical realist and a neorealist, respectively.[3] I shall also discuss some of the ideas of Thomas Hobbes and Niccolò Machiavelli, Western political theorists whose writings have had an important influence on contemporary realism. Of all the aca-

MAN, THE STATE, AND WAR

demic approaches to international relations, political realism is most closely associated with the worldview of foreign policy practitioners, particularly national security specialists. Realists have concentrated their investigations on the activities of the great powers: therefore my discussion in this section will be drawn mainly from the experiences of the great powers, particularly the contemporary United States with whose activities realists are centrally concerned.

For realists, security is tied to the military security of the state. Given their pessimistic assumptions about the likely behavior of states in an "anarchic" international environment, most realists are skeptical about the possibility of states ever achieving perfect security. In an imperfect world, where many states have national security interests that go beyond self-preservation and where there is no international government to curb their ambitions, realists tell us that war could break out at any time because nothing can prevent it. Consequently, they advise, states must rely on their own power capabilities to achieve security. The best contribution the discipline of international relations can make to national security is to investigate the causes of war and thereby help to design "realistic" policies that can prolong intervals of peace. Realists counsel that morality is usually ineffective in a dangerous world: a "realistic" understanding of amoral and instrumental behavior, characteristic of international politics, is necessary if states are not to fall prey to others' ambitions.

In looking for explanations for the causes of war, realists, as well as scholars in other approaches to international relations, have distinguished among three levels of analysis: the individual, the state, and the international system. While realists claim that their theories are "objective" and of universal validity, the assumptions they use when analyzing states and explaining their behavior in the international system are heavily dependent on characteristics that we, in the West, have come to associate with masculinity. The way in which realists describe the individual, the state, and the international system are profoundly gendered; each is constructed in terms of the idealized or hegemonic masculinity described in chapter 1. In the name of universality, realists have constructed a worldview based on the experiences of certain men: it is therefore a worldview that offers us only a partial view of reality.

Having examined the connection between realism and masculinity, I shall examine some feminist perspectives on national security. Using feminist theories, which draw on the experiences of women, I shall ask how it would affect the way in which we think about national security if we were to develop an alternative set of assumptions about the individual, the state, and the international system not based exclusively on the behavior of men. Realist assumptions about states as unitary actors render unproblematic the boundaries between anarchy and order and legitimate and illegitimate violence. If we were to include the experiences of women, how would it affect the way in which we understand the meaning of violence? While women have been less directly involved in international violence as soldiers, their lives have been affected by domestic violence in households, another unprotected space, and by the consequences of war and the policy priorities of militarized societies. Certain feminists have suggested that, because of what they see as a connection between sexism and militarism, violence at all levels of society is interrelated, a claim that calls into question the realist assumption of the anarchy/order distinction. Most important, these feminists claim that all types of violence are embedded in the gender hierarchies of dominance and subordination that I described in chapter 1. Hence they would argue that until these and other hierarchies associated with class and race are dismantled and until women have control over their own security a truly comprehensive system of security cannot be devised.

National Security and Contemporary Realism

Realist Prescriptions for National Security

Realists believe that, since there is no international government capable of enforcing impartial rules for states' behavior, states must take matters of security into their own hands even if it yields dangerous results. Kenneth Waltz uses eighteenth-century philosopher Jean-Jacques Rousseau's metaphor of a stag hunt to describe the likely security-seeking behavior of states given this condition of anarchy. Five hungry men agree to trap and share a stag, but when a hare runs by one man grabs it, thereby letting the stag escape: by defecting from the common goal, this hunter sacrifices the long-term cooperative interests of the group, his own included, for his immediate short-term interest.[4] For realists, this story illustrates the problematic nature of national security: in an international system of anarchy, rationality would dictate that mutual cooperation would work in the interest of all. But since men are self-seeking, politically ambitious, and not always rational, we must assume that some states and some men will not be cooperative and will start wars. Given the lack of an international government with powers of enforcement, states must therefore depend on themselves for their own security needs even if this is not in the best interests of the system as a whole.

For realists this is the classic security dilemma.[5] In an imperfect world states can never be sure of one another's intentions, so they arm themselves to achieve security; since this is an act that threatens someone else's security, it sets in motion a vicious cycle which results in the spiraling procurement of armaments and the possibility that war could break out at any time. Faced with the ever present threat of violence and the lack of a sanctioning authority to control it, how do realists suggest that states should act to promote peace and stability in such an environment?

Given their belief that perfect security is unattainable in

an imperfect world, realists believe that states can best opti-
mize their security through preparation for war. For Hans
Morgenthau, the security of the state is attained and pre-
served through the maximization of power, particularly military power. Elements of national power include secure geographical boundaries, large territorial size, the capacity for
self-sufficiency in natural and industrial resources, and a
strong technological base, all of which contribute to a strong
military capability.[6] Kenneth Waltz suggests that states can
enhance their security by following the principle of self-help:
in an anarchical international system, states must help themselves, for they can count on no one else to do so. For Waltz,
security depends on avoiding dependence and building the
capabilities necessary to defend against other states' aggressive acts: the greatest rewards for a state come, not from an
increase in well-being, which might be achieved through
heightened interdependence, but from the maintenance of
autonomy.[7] In a dangerous world, Waltz predicts that states
with the most power will be the most successful, because
power permits a wide range of action.

Prescriptions such as Morgenthau's power maximization
or Waltz's more ambiguously defined notion of self-help can
have dangerous consequences, given the conditions of anarchy and mutual distrust. In such an environment what prospects for peace and security that do exist rest on the operation of the balance of power, a mechanism that is crucial for
realist explanations of the behavior of states in the international system. Morgenthau claims that peace depends on
two mechanisms—balance of power and international law;
since he believes that depending solely on the latter is unrealistic, given the lack of any international enforcement
mechanism, peace will be maintained, although imperfectly,
by the balance of power. For realists, balance of power becomes an explanation of states' behavior as well as a device
for their self-preservation. While Morgenthau is somewhat
ambivalent as to whether states intentionally engage in power
balancing, Waltz claims that even if it is not the intention of

any one state, balances will form as states act, either alone or through alliances, to counter the power of others. Since alliances are often fragile and the power capabilities of states change, power balances tend toward instability. Given these uncertainties, Waltz claims that the bipolar balance of the Cold War period was more stable than multipolar systems. Not only did the United States and the Soviet Union check each others' actions without relying on alliance partners to increase their capabilities, but, in a bipolar world, each responded to unsettling events within clearly demarcated spheres of influence, thus maintaining stability throughout the system.[8]

In the post–World War II world, this bipolar balance of power became what less sanguine observers termed a "balance of terror" that rested on the vast array of nuclear weapons possessed by both the United States and the Soviet Union. In the United States, the unprecedented buildup and maintenance of huge military arsenals in a time of "peace" led to a new branch of international relations scholarship known as national security studies. While national security scholars are realists in their basic assumptions and explanations, during the Cold War era they focused almost exclusively on designing a military strategy for the United States with respect to the Soviet Union. As national security specialists have moved between academia and government, American national security policy has rested on the realist prescription of increasing security through preparation for war.

Strategic thinking has centered on the notion of deterrence, which means relying on one's strategic capability to prevent the enemy from attacking. From the 1960s until the end of the Cold War, the notion of mutual deterrence characterized the strategic relationship between the United States and the Soviet Union. The stability of mutual deterrence, a nuclear form of bipolar power-balancing, depends on second strike capability, the ability of both sides to destroy each others' homeland with nuclear weapons after either side has

33

launched a first attack. Although the United States and the Soviet Union engaged in a massive military buildup to preserve their security during the Cold War, ultimately that security rested on mutual vulnerability since neither side developed the defensive capability to resist the other's attack. However, strategists claim that this rough balance between the capabilities of each side was relatively stable because each side understood that to strike first would be to commit suicide. Even though realists have cautioned against the dangers of unpredictable actions by aggressive men and expansionist states, this argument in favor of strategic stability placed a great deal of emphasis on rationality, an emphasis prevalent in realist thinking more generally.

Realism's prescriptions for national security, described above, rest on the claims of its scholars that they are presenting a rational, objective assessment of the international system and the behavior of the states that constitute it. Labeling those who believe in the possibility of eliminating war through international law, international cooperation, or disarmament "idealists," realists claim that only through this "realistic" understanding of the nature of the international system can states undertake policies that will be successful in preserving their national security. Realists believe that explanations of states' behavior can be described in terms of laws that are objective, universal, and timeless. Politics, Morgenthau tells us, is governed by objective laws that have their roots in human nature; therefore it is possible to discover a rational theory that reflects these objective laws. Political realism, which for Morgenthau is the concept of interest defined in terms of power, stresses the rational, objective, and unemotional. Morgenthau claims that, in order to develop an autonomous theory of political behavior, "political man" must be abstracted from other aspects of human behavior. Political man is amoral; a failure to understand this drive to power, which is at the root of the behavior of both individuals and states, can be the pitfall of well-meaning statesmen whose attempts to act morally in the conduct of foreign relations can jeopardize the security of their own people.[9]

Since Morgenthau wrote the first edition of *Politics Among Nations* in 1948, the search for an objective, rational science of international politics based on models imported from economics and the natural sciences has been an important goal of the realist agenda. Neorealists, who have attempted to construct a positivist "science" of international relations, have used game theoretic and rational choice models in an effort to insert more scientific rigor into the field. Realists, as well as some of their critics, have also introduced the concept of "levels of analysis" to explore the causes of international wars more systematically. In international relations scholarship, causal explanations for war are conventionally situated at the levels of the individual, the state, or the international system.[10]

While most international relations literature concentrates on the second and third levels, neorealists, who are attempting to build more parsimonious and "scientific" approaches to the discipline, favor system-level explanations. Rejecting what he terms reductionist theories, Waltz claims that only at the level of the international system can we discover laws that can help us to understand the international behavior of states and the propensity for conflict. Waltz asserts that it is not possible to understand states' behavior simply by looking at each individual unit; one must look at the structure as a whole and see how each state's capabilities stand in relation to others'. The extent to which states will be successful in attaining their goals and providing for their own security can be predicted by analyzing their relative power capabilities. But given this self-seeking behavior in an anarchic environment, conflict is a likely outcome. Focusing his explanations at the level of the international system, Waltz claims that it is possible to observe regularities in the power-balancing behavior of states that can be explained in terms similar to those of equilibrium theory in microeconomics.[11]

A Gendered Perspective on National Security

Morgenthau, Waltz, and other realists claim that it is possible to develop a rational, objective theory of international politics based on universal laws that operate across time and space. In her feminist critique of the natural sciences, Evelyn Fox Keller points out that most scientific communities share the "assumption that the universe they study is directly accessible, represented by concepts shaped not by language but only by the demands of logic and experiment." The laws of nature, according to this view of science, are beyond the relativity of language.[12] Like most contemporary feminists, Keller rejects this positivist view of science that, she asserts, imposes a coercive, hierarchical, and conformist pattern on scientific inquiry. Since most contemporary feminist scholars believe that knowledge is socially constructed, they are skeptical of finding an unmediated foundation for knowledge that realists claim is possible. Since they believe that it is language that transmits knowledge, many feminists suggest that the scholarly claims about the neutral uses of language and about objectivity must continually be questioned.[13]

I shall now investigate the individual, the state, and the international system—the three levels of analysis that realists use in their analysis of war and national security—and examine how they have been constructed in realist discourse. I shall argue that the language used to describe these concepts comes out of a Western-centered historical worldview that draws almost exclusively on the experiences of men. Underneath its claim to universality this worldview privileges a view of security that is constructed out of values associated with hegemonic masculinity.

"Political Man"

In his *Politics Among Nations*, a text rich in historical detail, Morgenthau has constructed a world almost entirely without women. Morgenthau claims that individuals are engaged in a struggle for power whenever they come into contact with one another, for the tendency to dominate exists at all levels of human life: the family, the polity, and the international system; it is modified only by the conditions under which the struggle takes place.[14] Since women rarely occupy positions of power in any of these arenas, we can assume that, when Morgenthau talks about domination, he is talking primarily about men, although not all men.[15] His "political man" is a social construct based on a partial representation of human nature abstracted from the behavior of men in positions of public power.[16] Morgenthau goes on to suggest that, while society condemns the violent behavior that can result from this struggle for power within the polity, it encourages it in the international system in the form of war.

While Morgenthau's "political man" has been criticized by other international relations scholars for its essentializing view of human nature, the social construction of hegemonic masculinity and its opposition to a devalued femininity described in chapter 1, have been central to the way in which the discourse of international politics has been constructed more generally. In Western political theory from the Greeks to Machiavelli, traditions upon which contemporary realism relies heavily for its analysis, this socially constructed type of masculinity has been projected onto the international behavior of states. The violence with which it is associated has been legitimated through the glorification of war.

The militarized version of citizenship, similar to the "manly" behavior described in chapter 1, can be traced back to the ancient Greek city-states on whose history realists frequently draw in constructing their analysis. For the Greeks, the most honored way to achieve recognition as a citizen was through heroic performance and sacrifice in war. The real test of manly virtue or "arete," a militarized notion of greatness, was victory in battle.[17] The Greek city-state was a community of warriors. Women and slaves involved in the realm of "necessity" in the household or the economy were not included as citizens for they would pollute the higher realm of politics.[18]

This exclusive definition of the citizen-warrior reemerges in sixteenth-century Europe in the writings of Niccolò Machiavelli. Since he associates human excellence with the competitive striving for power, what is a negative but unavoidable characteristic of human nature for Morgenthau is a virtue for Machiavelli. Machiavelli translates this quest for power into the glorification of the warrior-prince whose prowess in battle was necessary for the salvation of his native Florence in the face of powerful external threats.

For feminists, warrior-citizenship is neither a negative, unavoidable characterization of human nature, nor a desirable possibility; it is a revisable, gendered construction of personality and citizenship. Feminist political theorist Wendy Brown suggests that Machiavelli's representation of the political world and its citizenry is profoundly gendered; it is dependent on an image of true manliness that demands qualities that are superior to those that naturally inhere in men.[19] Hannah Pitkin claims that for Machiavelli triumph in war, honor and liberty in civic life, and independent critical thought and manliness in personal relationships are all bound together by a central preoccupation with autonomy, a characteristic associated with masculinity.[20] True manliness, demanded of the ideal citizen-warrior, is encompassed in the concept "virtu," which means, in its literal sense, manly activity. For Machiavelli, virtu is insight, energetic activity, effectiveness, and courage: it demands overcoming a man's self-indulgence and laziness.[21]

Just as the concept of hegemonic masculinity, described in chapter 1, requires for its construction an oppositional relationship to a devalued femininity, Machiavelli's construction of the citizen-warrior required a similarly devalued "other" against which true manhood and autonomy could be set. In Machiavelli's writings this feminine other is "fortuna," originally a Roman goddess associated with capriciousness and unpredictability. Hannah Pitkin claims that in Machiavelli's writings fortuna is presented as the feminine power in men themselves against which they must continually struggle to maintain their autonomy.[22] In the public world, Machiavelli depicts fortuna as chance, situations that could not have been foreseen or that men fail to control. The capriciousness of fortuna cannot be prevented, but it can be prepared against and overcome through the cultivation of manly virtues. According to Brown, fortuna and virtu are in permanent combat: both are supremely gendered constructions that involve a notion of manliness that is tied to the conquest of women.[23] In Machiavelli's own words, "Fortune is a woman, and it is necessary if you wish to master her, to conquer her by force."[24]

Having constructed these explicitly gendered representations of virtu and fortuna, Machiavelli also makes it clear that he considers women to be a threat to the masculinity of the citizen-warrior. Although they scarcely appear in Machiavelli's political writings, when women are discussed, Machiavelli portrays them as both dangerous and inferior.[25] The most dangerous threat to both a man *and* a state is to be like a women because women are weak, fearful, indecisive, and dependent—stereotypes that, as described in chapter 1, still surface when assessing women's suitability for the military and the conduct of foreign policy today.

While contemporary international relations does not employ this explicitly misogynist discourse, the contemporary understanding of citizenship still remains bound up with the Greeks' and Machiavelli's depictions of the citizen-warrior. The most noble sacrifice a citizen can make is to give his life for his country. When the National Organization for Women decided to support the drafting of women into the United States military, it argued its case on the grounds that, if women were barred from participation in the armed forces on an equal footing with men, they would remain second-class citizens denied the unique political responsibility of risking one's life for the state.[26] But in spite of women's increasing numbers in noncombat roles in the armed forces of certain states, the relationship between soldiering, masculinity, and citizenship remains very strong in most societies today.

To be a soldier is to be a man, not a woman; more than any other social institution, the military separates men from women. Soldiering is a role into which boys are socialized in school and on the playing fields. A soldier must be a protector; he must show courage, strength, and responsibility and repress feelings of fear, vulnerability, and compassion. Such feelings are womanly traits, which are liabilities in time of war.[27] War demands manliness; it is an event in which boys become men, for combat is the ultimate test of masculinity. When women become soldiers, this gender identity is called into question; for Americans, this questioning became real during the Persian Gulf war of 1991, the first time that women soldiers were sent into a war zone in large numbers.[28]

To understand the citizen-warrior as a social construction allows us to question the essentialist connection between war and men's natural aggressiveness. Considerable evidence suggests that most men would prefer not to fight; many refuse to do so even when they are put in positions that make it difficult not to. One study shows that in World War II, on the average, only 15 percent of soldiers actually fired their weapons in battle, even when threatened by enemy soldiers.[29] Because military recruiters cannot rely on violent qualities in men, they appeal to manliness and patriotic duty. Judith Stiehm avers that military trainers resort to manipulation of men's anxiety about their sexual identity in order to increase soldiers' willingness to fight. In basic training the term of utmost derision is to be called a girl or a lady.[30] The association between men and violence therefore depends not on men's innate aggressiveness, but on the construction of a gendered identity that places heavy pressure on soldiers to prove themselves as men.

Just as the Greeks gave special respect to citizens who had proved themselves in war, it is still a special mark of respect in many societies to be a war veteran, an honor that is denied to all women as well as to certain men. In the United States, nowhere is this more evident than in the political arena where "political man's" identity is importantly tied to his service in the military. Sheila Tobias suggests that there are risks involved for politicians seeking office who have chosen not to serve in combat or for women who cannot serve. War service is of special value for gaining votes even in political offices not exclusively concerned with foreign policy. In the United States, former generals are looked upon favorably as presidential candidates, and many American presidents have run for office on their war record. In the 1984 vice presidential debates between George Bush and Geraldine Ferraro, Bush talked about his experience as a navy pilot shot down in World War II; while this might seem like a dubious qualification for the office of vice president, it was one that Ferraro—to her detriment—could not counter.[31]

To be a first-class citizen therefore, one must be a warrior. It is an important qualification for the politics of national security for it is to such men that the state entrusts its most vital interests. Characteristics associated with femininity are considered a liability when dealing with the realities of international politics. When realists write about national security, they often do so in abstract and depersonalized terms, yet they are constructing a discourse shaped out of these gendered identities. This notion of manhood, crucial for upholding the interests of the state, is an image that is frequently extended to the way in which we personify the behavior of the state itself.

The Masculine State

" 'To Saddam,' Mr. Cheney wrote on the 2,000 pound bomb destined for an Iraqi target. 'With appreciation, Dick Cheney.' "[32] In times of war, the state itself becomes a citizen-warrior: military commanders refer to the enemy as a singular "he." The 1991 Persian Gulf war was frequently depicted as a personal contest between Saddam Hussein and George

Bush and described in the appropriate locker-room or foot-ball language.[33] When realists describe the international be-havior of states more generally, they present us with simi-larly masculine images of stag hunts or "games nations play."[34] Hans Morgenthau described the Soviet-American rivalry of the early Cold War period as "the primitive spec-tacle of two giants eying each other with watchful suspicion. . . . Both prepare to strike the first decisive blow, for if one does not strike it the other might."[35]

More recently, however, neorealism has depicted states rather differently, as abstract unitary actors whose actions are explained through laws that can be universalized across time and place and whose internal characteristics are irrele-vant to the operation of these laws. States appear to act according to some higher rationality that is presented as independent of human agency. Nowhere in the rational power-balancing behavior of states can we find the patriot willing to go to war to defend his women and children in the name of national security. As poststructuralist international relations theorist Richard Ashley suggests, the "rationaliza-tion of global politics" has led to an antihumanism whereby states, posited unproblematically as unitary actors, act inde-pendently of human interests.[36] It is a world in which, as Jean Elshtain observes, "No children are ever born, and nobody ever dies. . . . There are states, and they are what is."[37]

Behind this reification of state practices hide social institu-tions that are made and remade by individual actions. In reality, the neorealist depiction of the state as a unitary actor is grounded in the historical practices of the Western state system: neorealist characterizations of state behavior, in terms of self-help, autonomy, and power seeking, privilege char-acteristics associated with the Western construction of mas-culinity. Since the beginning of the state system, the national security functions of states have been deeded to us through gendered images that privilege masculinity.

The Western state system began in seventeenth-century

Europe. As described by Charles Tilly, the modern state was born through war; leaders of nascent states consolidated their power through the coercive extraction of resources and the conquest of ever-larger territories. Success in war continued to be imperative for state survival and the building of state apparatus.[38] Throughout the period of state building in the West, nationalist movements have used gendered imagery that exhorts masculine heroes to fight for the establishment and defense of the mother country. The collective identity of citizens in most states depends heavily on telling stories about, and celebration of, wars of independence or national liberation and other great victories in battle. National anthems are frequently war songs, just as holidays are celebrated with military parades and uniforms that recall great feats in past conflicts. These collective historical memories are very important for the way in which individuals define themselves as citizens as well as for the way in which states command support for their policies, particularly foreign policy. Rarely, however, do they include experiences of women or female heroes.

While the functions of twentieth-century states extend well beyond the provision of national security, national security issues, particularly in time of war, offer a sense of shared political purpose lacking in most other areas of public policy.[39] The state continues to derive much of its legitimacy from its security function; it is for national security that citizens are willing to make sacrifices, often unquestioningly.[40] Military budgets are the least likely area of public spending to be contested by politicians and the public, who are often manipulated into supporting military spending by linking it with patriotism. When we think about the state acting in matters of national security, we are entering a policy world almost exclusively inhabited by men. Men make national security policy both inside and outside the military establishment.

In the United States, women have entered the military primarily in the lower ranks. Despite growing numbers of women in the U.S. military, which at present has the largest percentage of women of any military establishment, it remains a male institution. According to an internal review at the United States Naval Academy fourteen years after the first woman was admitted, reported in the *New York Times* of October 10, 1990, a considerable segment of midshipmen, faculty, and staff believed that women have no place there.[41] Judith Stiehm suggests that American military leaders think of the armed services as "belonging" to men whereas in reality they belong to citizens, more than half of whom are women.[42] When women enter the military, their position is ambiguous; men do not want women fighting alongside them, and the public perceives the role of wife and mother as less compatible with being a soldier than that of husband and father. While modern technology blurs the distinction between combat and noncombat roles, women are still barred from combat roles in all militaries, and the functions that women perform are less rewarded than those of the fighting forces.[43] Joining the debate in the United States in 1991 over women's suitability for combat, retired U.S. General Robert Barrow declared, "Women give life, sustain life, nurture life. . . . If you want to make a combat unit ineffective, assign women to it."[44]

In the nuclear age military strategy must be planned in peacetime, since it is hypothesized that there would be no time to plan a strategy that involves the use of nuclear weapons once war has broken out. Nuclear strategy is constructed by civilian national security specialists, far removed from public debate, in a language that, while it is too esoteric for most people to understand, claims to be rational and objective. Carol Cohn argues that strategic discourse, with its emphasis on strength, stability, and rationality, bears an uncanny resemblance to the ideal image of masculinity. Critics of U.S. nuclear strategy are branded as irrational and emotional. In the United States, these "defense intellectuals" are almost all white men; Cohn tells us that while their language is one of abstraction, it is loaded with sexual imagery.[45] She claims that the discourse employed in professional and political debates about U.S. security policy "would appear to have colonized our minds and to have subjugated other ways of understanding relations among states."[46] Cohn suggests that this discourse has become the only legitimate response to questions of how best to achieve national security; it is a discourse far removed from politics and people, and its deliberations go on disconnected from the functions they are supposed to serve. Its powerful claim to legitimacy rests, in part, on the way national security specialists view the international system.

The International System: The War of Everyman Against Everyman

According to Richard Ashley, realists have privileged a higher reality called "the sovereign state" against which they have posited anarchy understood in a negative way as difference, ambiguity, and contingency—as a space that is external and dangerous.[47] All these characteristics have also been attributed to women. Anarchy is an actual or potential site of war. The most common metaphor that realists employ to describe the anarchical international system is that of the seventeenth-century English philosopher Thomas Hobbes's depiction of the state of nature. Although Hobbes did not write much about international politics, realists have applied his description of individuals' behavior in a hypothetical precontractual state of nature, which Hobbes termed the war of everyman against everyman, to the behavior of states in the international system.[48]

Carole Pateman argues that, in all contemporary discussions of the state of nature, the differentiation between the sexes is generally ignored, even though it was an important consideration for contract theorists themselves.[49] Although Hobbes did suggest that women as well as men could be free and equal individuals in the state of nature, his description of human behavior in this environment refers to that of adult males whose behavior is taken as constitutive of human nature as a whole by contemporary realist analysis. According to Jane Flax, the individuals that Hobbes described in the state of nature appeared to come to full maturity without any engagement with one another; they were solitary creatures lacking any socialization in interactive behavior. Any interactions they did have led to power struggles that resulted in domination or submission. Suspicion of others' motives led to behavior characterized by aggression, self-interest, and the drive for autonomy.[50] In a similar vein, Christine Di Stephano uses feminist psychoanalytic theory to support her claim that the masculine dimension of atomistic egoism is powerfully underscored in Hobbes's state of nature, which, she asserts, is built on the foundation of denied maternity. "Hobbes' abstract man is a creature who is self-possessed and radically solitary in a crowded and inhospitable world, whose relations with others are unavoidably contractual and whose freedom consists in the absence of impediments to the attainment of privately generated and understood desires."[51]

As a model of human behavior, Hobbes's depiction of individuals in the state of nature is partial at best; certain feminists have argued that such behavior could be applicable only to adult males, for if life was to go on for more than one generation in the state of nature, women must have been involved in activities such as reproduction and child rearing rather than in warfare. Reproductive activities require an environment that can provide for the survival of infants and behavior that is interactive and nurturing.

An international system that resembles Hobbes's state of nature is a dangerous environment. Driven by competition for scarce resources and mistrust of others' motives in a system that lacks any legitimate authority, states, like men, must rely on their own resources for self-preservation.[52] Machiavelli offers advice to his prince that is based on similar assumptions about the international system. Both Pitkin and Brown note that Machiavelli's portrayal of fortuna is regularly associated with nature, as something outside the political world that must be subdued and controlled. Pitkin refers to "The Golden Ass," a long unfinished poem by Machiavelli, based on the legend of Circe, a female figure who lives in the forest world and turns men into animals.[53] Translated into international politics this depiction of fortuna is similar to the disorder or anarchy of the international system as portrayed by realists. Capturing the essence of Realpolitik, Brown suggests that, for Machiavelli, politics is a continual quest for power and independence; it is dependent on the presence of an enemy at all times, for without spurs to greatness energized by fighting an enemy, the polity would collapse.

Just as the image of waging war against an exterior other figured centrally in Machiavelli's writings, war is central to the way we learn about international relations. Our historical memories of international politics are deeded to us through wars as we mark off time periods in terms of intervals between conflicts. We learn that dramatic changes take place in the international system after major wars when the relative power of states changes. Wars are fought for many reasons; yet, frequently, the rationale for fighting wars is presented in gendered terms such as the necessity of standing up to aggression rather then being pushed around or appearing to be a sissy or a wimp. Support for wars is often garnered through the appeal to masculine characteristics. As Sara Ruddick states, while the masculinity of war may be a myth, it is one that sustains both women and men in their support for violence.[54] War is a time when male and female characteristics become polarized; it is a gendering activity at a time when the discourse of militarism and masculinity permeates the whole fabric of society.[55]

As Jean Elshtain points out, war is an experience to which women are exterior; men have inhabited the world of war in a way that women have not.[56] The history of international politics is therefore a history from which women are, for the most part, absent. Little material can be found on women's roles in wars; generally they are seen as victims, rarely as agents. While war can be a time of advancement for women as they step in to do men's jobs, the battlefront takes precedence, so the hierarchy remains and women are urged to step aside once peace is restored. When women themselves engage in violence, it is often portrayed as a mob or a food riot that is out of control.[57] Movements for peace, which are also part of our history, have not been central to the conventional way in which the evolution of the Western state system has been presented to us. International relations scholars of the early twentieth century, who wrote positively about the possibilities of international law and the collective security system of the League of Nations, were labeled "idealists" and not taken seriously by the more powerful realist tradition.

Metaphors, such as Hobbes's state of nature are primarily concerned with representing conflictual relations between great powers. The images used to describe nineteenth-century imperialist projects and contemporary great power relations with former colonial states are somewhat different. Historically, colonial people were often described in terms that drew on characteristics associated with women in order to place them lower in a hierarchy that put their white male colonizers on top. As the European state system expanded outward to conquer much of the world in the nineteenth century, its "civilizing" mission was frequently described in stereotypically gendered terms. Colonized peoples were often described as being effeminate, masculinity was an attribute of the white man, and colonial order depended on Victorian standards of manliness. Cynthia Enloe suggests that the concept of "ladylike behavior" was one of the mainstays of imperialist civilization. Like sanitation and Christianity, feminine respectability was meant to convince colonizers and colonized alike that foreign conquest was right and necessary. Masculinity denoted protection of the respectable lady; she stood for the civilizing mission that justified the colonization of benighted peoples.[58] Whereas the feminine stood

for danger and disorder for Machiavelli, the European female, in contrast to her colonial counterpart, came to represent a stable, civilized order in nineteenth-century representations of British imperialism.

An example of the way in which these gender identities
were manipulated to justify Western policy with respect to
the rest of the world can also be seen in attitudes toward
Latin America prevalent in the United States in the nineteenth century. According to Michael Hunt, nineteenth-century American images of Latin society depicted a (usually
black) male who was lazy, dishonest, and corrupt. A con-
trary image that was more positive—a Latin as redeemable—
took the form of a fair-skinned senorita living in a marginalized society, yet escaping its degrading effects. Hunt suggests that Americans entered the twentieth century with
three images of Latin America fostered through legends
brought back by American merchants and diplomats. These
legends, perpetuated through school texts, cartoons, and
political rhetoric, were even incorporated into the views of
policymakers. The three images pictured the Latin as a half-
breed brute, feminized, or infantile. In each case, Americans
stood superior; the first image permitted a predatory aggressiveness, the second allowed the United States to assume
the role of ardent suitor, and the third justified America's
need to provide tutelage and discipline. All these images are
profoundly gendered: the United States as a civilizing warrior, a suitor, or a father, and Latin America as a lesser male,
a female, or a child.[59]

Such images, although somewhat muted, remain today
and are particularly prevalent in the thinking of Western
states when they are dealing with the Third World. In the
post–World War II era, there was considerable debate in
Western capitals about the dangers of premature independence for primitive peoples. In the postindependence era,
former colonial states and their leaders have frequently been
portrayed as emotional and unpredictable, characteristics also
associated with women. C. D. Jackson, an adviser to Presi-

dent Eisenhower and a patron of Western development theorists in the 1950s, evoked these feminine characteristics when
he observed that "the Western world has somewhat more
experience with the operations of war, peace, and parlia-
mentary procedures than the swirling mess of emotionally
super-charged Africans and Asiatics and Arabs that outnumber us."[60]

According to Hunt, Eisenhower himself regarded the En-
glish-speaking people of the world as superior to all the rest;
thus they provided a model for right behavior in the international system. This idea is not incompatible with contemporary realism, which, while it has been an approach dominated by white Anglo-Saxon men, has prescribed the behavior of states throughout the international system. As we have
witnessed the enormous buildup of nuclear weapons on the
part of the United States and the former Soviet Union beyond any level that could be considered "rational," our policymakers caution that only a few of these same weapons in
the hands of people in the Third World pose a greater threat
to world security.

In this section, I have shown how realists paint a consistent three-tiered picture of a world in which survival in a
violence-prone international system "requires" war-capable
states peopled by heroic masculine citizen-warriors. This picture legitimates certain "realistic" portrayals of situations
and conduct at each level, which serve to reinforce the need
for power balancing, strong states, and citizen-warriors. It
achieves relative consistency by downplaying the feasibility
and attractiveness of alternative possibilities at each level of
analysis by claiming that peaceful international systems are
idealist utopias, that non–power-seeking states are soon
conquered or dismembered, and that citizens who are not
warriors are inessential to the reproduction of the state.

Feminist perspectives should question the analytical separability of these three levels of analysis, which realists have
treated as supposedly independent levels or aspects of reality. If systems-oriented realists criticize reductionist causal

accounts focused only on human nature, feminists might equally well object that scientific causal analyses of state and system-level phenomena distract our attention from the role of responsible individuals and groups in the construction and maintenance of state-level and systemic relationships. Power-oriented statesmen have a vested interest vis-à-vis their domestic supporters in painting a picture of the world around them as threateningly anarchic; anarchic international systems are reproduced by individuals who believe no alternatives exist.

Recognizing the gendered construction of this three-tiered world picture, feminist perspectives on national security must offer alternative conceptions. Assuming that these categories are mutually constitutive and mutually reinforcing of each other, we should heed Paul Fussell's claim, in the epigraph to this chapter, that our conception of the possibilities of individual manhood must be redefined in theory and practice before war at the international systemic level can be regarded as avoidable. These gendered depictions of political man, the state, and the international system generate a national security discourse that privileges conflict and war and silences other ways of thinking about security; moving away from valorizing human characteristics that are associated with the risking of life, toward an affirmation of life-giving qualities, allows us to envisage alternative conceptions of national security.

National Security Reconsidered

Certain critics of realism have begun to ask whether we can continue to rely on war as the ultimate instrument for the achievement of national security. In a world where nuclear conflict could result in the destruction of winners and losers alike (as well as the natural environment), realist prescriptions to maximize power could actually be counterproductive. In the absence of a viable defense, nuclear weapons make boundary protection impossible; thus the distinctions between domestic and international, soldiers and civilians, and protectors and protected are breaking down.[61] In 1982 the Independent Commission on Disarmament and Security Issues warned that, after thirty-seven years, nuclear deterrence was becoming fragile because of a decreased sensitivity to dangers, the possibility of accidents in crisis situations, and new technologies that may be increasing the possibility of limited nuclear war.[62] In the nuclear age, the fact that the security of states depends on the insecurity of their citizens has stretched the traditional concept of national security to its limit.

Critics of realism argue that a more global vision of security is necessary. The extent to which realism has been able to justify its distinction between domestic order and international anarchy depends on its focus on the major actors in the international system. Internally, most Western states have been relatively peaceful since World War II, if peace is narrowly defined as the absence of military conflict. Thinking about security from a global perspective must take into account that 90 percent of the military conflicts of the 1970s and 1980s took place in the Third World; many were domestic, some international and some, particularly when the great powers were involved, blurred the distinction between the two.[63] Security threats have traditionally been defined as threats to national boundaries, but since the end of the process of decolonialization, relatively few cross-border wars and changes in international boundaries have occurred, in spite of the large number of military conflicts. For people in the Third World, as well as in Eastern Europe and, more recently, in the states of the former Soviet Union, security threats have often been internal. Repression by regimes reacting against ethnic minorities or popular discontent creates a situation in which states can become threats to, rather than providers of, security. The militarization of much of the Third World, often with weapons supplied by great powers whose interests frequently coincide with keeping unpopular re-

gimes in power, has led to the legitimation of states frequently depending on their recognition by the international
community rather-than by their domestic populations.[64] These
trends, together with the winding down of some significant
international conflicts in the late 1980s, suggest that we may
be moving toward a system characterized by international
order and domestic disorder, a situation that could turn the
traditional notion of national security on its head.

Acknowledging these multiple sources of insecurity, various new thinkers have come up with very different definitions of security. In the introduction to the Report of the
Independent Commission on Disarmament and Security Issues, Olof Palme defines security in terms of joint survival
rather than mutual destruction.[65] The commission defines
what it calls "common security" in terms that extend well
beyond nuclear strategic issues. It looks at security in North-
South as well as East-West terms; focusing on military conflict in the Third World, new thinking points to possible
contradictions between the military security of states and the
economic well-being of their citizens. The Palme Report notes
that a growing militarization of the Third World has drained
resources that might otherwise be used for economic development.

When we consider security from the perspective of the
individual, we find that new thinking is beginning to provide us with definitions of security that are less state-centered and less militaristic. But little attention has been paid
either to gender issues or to women's particular needs with
respect to security or to their contributions toward its
achievement. Feminist reformulations of the meaning of security are needed to draw attention to the extent to which
gender hierarchies themselves are a source of domination
and thus an obstacle to a truly comprehensive definition of
security. I shall now turn to the issue of how women might
define national security and to an analysis of security from a
feminist perspective.

Feminist Perspectives on National Security
Women Define Security

It is difficult to find definitions by women of national security. While it is not necessarily the case that women have not had ideas on this subject, they are not readily accessible in the literature of international relations. When women speak or write about national security, they are often dismissed as being naive or unrealistic. An example of this is the women in the United States and Europe who spoke out in the early years of the century for a more secure world order. Addressing the International Congress of Women at the Hague during World War I, Jane Addams spoke of the need for a new internationalism to replace the self-destructive nationalism that contributed so centrally to the outbreak and mass destruction of that war. Resolutions adopted at the close of the congress questioned the assumption that women, and civilians more generally, could be protected during modern war. The conference concluded that assuring security through military means was no longer possible owing to the indiscriminate nature of modern warfare, and it called for disarmament as a more appropriate course for ensuring future security.[66]

At the Women's International Peace Conference in Halifax, Canada, in 1985, a meeting of women from all over the world, participants defined security in various ways depending on the most immediate threats to their survival; security meant safe working conditions and freedom from the threat of war or unemployment or the economic squeeze of foreign debt. Discussions of the meaning of security revealed divisions between Western middle-class women's concerns with nuclear war, concerns that were similar to those of Jane Addams and her colleagues, and Third World women who defined insecurity more broadly in terms of the structural violence associated with imperialism, militarism, racism, and sexism. Yet all agreed that security meant nothing if it was built on others' insecurity.[67]

The final document of the World Conference to Review and Appraise the Achievements of the United Nations Decade for Women, held in Nairobi in 1985, offered a similarly multidimensional definition of security. The introductory chapter of the document defined peace as "not only the absence of war, violence and hostilities at the national and international levels but also the enjoyment of economic and social justice."[68] All these definitions of security take issue with realists' assumptions that security is zero-sum and must therefore be built on the insecurity of others.

Jane Addams's vision of national security, which deemphasizes its military dimension and was dismissed at the time as impractical, is quite compatible with the new thinking on common security I have just described. Like women at the Halifax and Nairobi conferences, contemporary new thinkers also include the elimination of structural violence in their definition of security. Feminist peace researcher Elise Boulding tells us that women peace researchers were among the pioneers in this contemporary redefinition of security, although, like Jane Addams at the beginning of the century, their work did not receive the attention it deserved. It is often the case that new ideas in any discipline do not receive widespread attention unless they are adopted by significant numbers of men, in which case women's work tends to become invisible through co-optation. Boulding claims that the one area in which women are not in danger of co-optation is their analysis of patriarchy and the linkage of war to violence against women.[69] Like most other feminists, Boulding believes that these issues must also be included in any comprehensive definition of security.

Given these various definitions of security offered by women, it is evident that feminist perspectives on security would grow out of quite different assumptions about the individual, the state, and the international system. Using feminist literature from various disciplines and approaches I shall now suggest what some of these perspectives might look like.

Reexamining the Anarchy/Order Distinction

The pervasiveness of internal conflict within states in the latter part of the twentieth century and the threats that militarized states pose to their own populations have called into question the realist assumption about the anarchy/order distinction. Critics of realism have also questioned the unitary actor assumption that renders the domestic affairs of states unproblematic when talking about their international behavior. Claiming that militarism, sexism, and racism are interconnected, most feminists would agree that the behavior of individuals and the domestic policies of states cannot be separated from states' behavior in the international system.[70] Feminists call attention to the particular vulnerabilities of women within states, vulnerabilities that grow out of hierarchical gender relations that are also interrelated with international politics. Calling into question the notion of the "protected," the National Organization for Women in their "Resolution on Women in Combat" of September 16, 1990, estimated that 80–90 percent of casualties due to conflict since World War II have been civilians, the majority of whom have been women and children. In militarized societies women are particularly vulnerable to rape, and evidence suggests that domestic violence is higher in military families or in families that include men with prior military service. Even though most public violence is committed by men against other men, it is more often women who feel threatened in public places.[71] Jill Radford suggests that when women feel it is unsafe to go out alone, their equal access to job opportunities is limited.[72] Studies also show that violence against women increases during hard economic times; when states prioritize military spending or find themselves in debt, shrinking resources are often accompanied by violence against women.

Feminist theories draw our attention to another anarchy/ order distinction—the boundary between a public domestic space protected, at least theoretically, by the rule of law and the private space of the family where, in many cases, no such legal protection exists. In most states domestic violence is not considered a concern of the state, and even when it is, law enforcement officials are often unwilling to get involved. Domestic assaults on women, often seen as "victim precipitated," are not taken as seriously as criminal assaults. Maria Mies argues that the modernization process in the Third World, besides sharpening class conflict, has led to an increase in violence against women in the home as traditional social values are broken down. While poor women probably suffer the most from family violence, a growing women's movement in India points to an increase in violence against educated middle-class women also, the most extreme form of which is dowry murder when young brides are found dead in suspicious circumstances. Eager to marry off their daughters, families make promises for dowries that exceed their means and that they are subsequently unable to pay.[73] In 1982 there were 332 cases of "accidental burning" of women in New Delhi; many more cases of "dowry deaths" go unreported.[74]

Recent studies of family violence in the United States and Western Europe have brought to light similar problems. When the family is violence-prone, it is frequently beyond the reach of the law; citing a 1978 report of the California Commission on the Status of Women, Pauline Gee documents that in 1978 one-quarter of the murders in the United States occurred within the family, one-half of these being husband-wife killings. Much of this family violence takes place outside the sanction of the legal system; it has been estimated that only 2 percent of men who beat their wives or female living partners are ever prosecuted.[75]

Maria Mies argues that this line, which demarcates public and private, separates state-regulated violence, the rule of right for which there are legally sanctioned punishments, and male violence, the rule of might for which, in many societies, no such legal sanctions exist. The rule of might and the rule of right are descriptions that have also been used in international relations discourse to distinguish the international and domestic spheres. By drawing our attention to the frequently forgotten realm of family violence that is often beyond the reach of the law, these feminists point to the interrelationship of violence and oppression across all levels of analysis. Feminist perspectives on security would assume that violence, whether it be in the international, national, or family realm, is interconnected.[76] Family violence must be seen in the context of wider power relations; it occurs within a gendered society in which male power dominates at all levels.[77] If men are traditionally seen as protectors, an important aspect of this role is protecting women against certain men.[78] Any feminist definition of security must therefore include the elimination of all types of violence, including violence produced by gender relations of domination and subordination. The achievement of this comprehensive vision of security requires a rethinking of the way in which citizenship has traditionally been defined, as well as alternative models for describing the behavior of states in the international system.

Citizenship Redefined

Building on the notion of hegemonic masculinity, the notion of the citizen-warrior depends on a devalued femininity for its construction. In international relations, this devalued femininity is bound up with myths about women as victims in need of protection; the protector/protected myth contributes to the legitimation of a militarized version of citizenship that results in unequal gender relations that can precipitate violence against women. Certain feminists have called for the construction of an enriched version of citizenship that would depend less on military values and more on an equal recognition of women's contributions to society. Such a notion of citizenship cannot come about, however, until myths that perpetuate views of women as victims rather than agents are eliminated.

One such myth is the association of women with peace, an association that has been invalidated through considerable evidence of women's support for men's wars in many societies.[79] In spite of a gender gap, a plurality of women generally support war and national security policies; Bernice Carroll suggests that the association of women and peace is one that has been imposed on women by their disarmed condition.[80] In the West, this association grew out of the Victorian ideology of women's moral superiority and the glorification of motherhood. This ideal was expressed by feminist Charlotte Perkins Gilman whose book *Herland* was first serialized in *The Forerunner* in 1915. Gilman glorified women as caring and nurturing mothers whose private sphere skills could benefit the world at large.[81] Most turn-of-the-century feminists shared Gilman's ideas. But if the implication of this view was that women were disqualified from participating in the corrupt world of political and economic power by virtue of their moral superiority, the result could only be the perpetuation of male dominance. Many contemporary feminists see dangers in the continuation of these essentializing myths that can only result in the perpetuation of women's subordination and reinforce dualisms that serve to make men more powerful. The association of femininity with peace lends support to an idealized masculinity that depends on constructing women as passive victims in need of protection. It also contributes to the claim that women are naive in matters relating to international politics. An enriched, less militarized notion of citizenship cannot be built on such a weak foundation.

While women have often been willing to support men's wars, many women are ambivalent about fighting in them, often preferring to leave that task to men. Feminists have also been divided on this issue; some argue, on the grounds of equality, that women must be given equal access to the military, while others suggest that women must resist the draft in order to promote a politics of peace. In arguing for women's equal access to the military, Judith Stiehm proposes that a society composed of citizens equally likely to experience violence and be responsible for its exercise would be stronger and more desirable. Stiehm claims that if everyone, women and men alike, were protectors, less justification for immoral acts would be found; with less emphasis on the manliness of war, new questions about its morality could be raised.[82] She suggests that women's enhanced role in the military could lead to a new concept of citizen-defender rather than warrior-patriot.

Just as the notion of a soldier as a wife and mother changes our image of soldiering, citizen-defenders change our image of war. Citizen-defenders are quite compatible with what Stephen Nathanson, in his redefinition of the meaning of patriotism, calls a moderate patriot. Rather than the traditional view of patriotism built on aggression and war, Nathanson suggests thinking of patriotism as support for one's own nation while not inflicting harm on others.[83] Such patriotism could be consistent with a defensive strategy in war if everyone were to comply.

Discarding the association between women and pacifism allows us to think of women as activists for the kind of change needed to achieve the multidimensional security I have already discussed. Even if not all women are pacifists, peace is an issue that women can support in their various roles as mothers, war victims, and preservers of states' and the world's good health.[84] Women at Greenham Common demonstrating against the installation of cruise missiles in Britain in 1981 came to see themselves as strong, brave, and creative—experiences frequently confined to men.[85] The Madres de la Plaza de Mayo, demonstrating during the 1980s in support of those who had disappeared in Argentina during the military dictatorship, experienced similar empowerment. Sara Ruddick suggests conscripting women in the interests of peace; Ruddick claims that while caring for children is not "natural" for women, it has been a womanly practice in most societies and one that she believes is an important resource for peace politics.[86] Ruddick defines maternal thinking as focused on the preservation of life and the growth of children. Maternal practice requires the peaceful settlement of disputes; since she feels that it is a mode of thinking to be found in men as well as women, it is one that could be useful for a politics of peace were it to be validated in the public realm.

In spite of many women's support for men's wars, a consistent gender gap in voting on defense-related issues in many countries suggests that women are less supportive of policies that rest on the use of direct violence. Before the outbreak of the Persian Gulf war in 1990, women in the United States were overwhelmingly against the use of force and, for the first time, women alone turned the public opinion polls against opting for war.[87] During the 1980s, when the Reagan administration was increasing defense budgets, women were less likely to support defense at the expense of social programs, a pattern that, in the United States, holds true for women's behavior more generally.

Explanations for this gender gap, which in the United States appears to be increasing as time goes on, range from suggestions that women have not been socialized into the practice of violence to claims that women are increasingly voting their own interests. While holding down jobs, millions of women also care for children, the aged, and the sick—activities that usually take place outside the economy. When more resources go to the military, additional burdens are placed on such women as public sector resources for social services shrink. While certain women are able, through access to the military, to give service to their country, many more are serving in these traditional care-giving roles. A feminist challenge to the traditional definition of patriotism should therefore question the meaning of service to one's country.[88] In contrast to a citizenship that rests on the assumption that it is more glorious to die than to live for one's state, Wendy Brown suggests that a more constructive view of citizenship could center on the courage to sustain life.[89] In similar terms, Jean Elshtain asserts the need to move toward a politics that shifts the focus of political loyalty and identity from sacrifice to responsibility.[90] Only when women's contributions to society are seen as equal to men's can these reconstructed visions of citizenship come about.

Feminist Perspectives on States' Security-Seeking Behavior

Realists have offered us an instrumental version of states' security-seeking behavior, which, I have argued, depends on a partial representation of human behavior associated with a stereotypical hegemonic masculinity. Feminist redefinitions of citizenship allow us to envisage a less militarized version of states' identities, and feminist theories can also propose alternative models for states' international security-seeking behavior, extrapolated from a more comprehensive view of human behavior.

Realists use state-of-nature stories as metaphors to describe the insecurity of states in an anarchical international system. I shall suggest an alternative story, which could equally be applied to the behavior of individuals in the state of nature. Although frequently unreported in standard historical accounts, it is a true story, not a myth, about a state of nature in early nineteenth-century America. Among those present in the first winter encampment of the 1804–1806 Lewis and Clark expedition into the Northwest territories was Sacajawea, a member of the Shoshone tribe. Sacajawea had joined the expedition as the wife of a French interpreter; her presence was proving invaluable to the security of the expedition's members, whose task it was to explore uncharted territory and establish contact with the native inhabitants to inform them of claims to these territories by the United States. Although unanticipated by its leaders, the presence of a woman served to assure the native inhabitants that the expedition was peaceful since the Native Americans assumed that war parties would not include women: the expedition was therefore safer because it was not armed.[91]

This story demonstrates that the introduction of women can change the way humans are assumed to behave in the state of nature. Just as Sacajawea's presence changed the Native American's expectations about the behavior of intruders into their territory, the introduction of women into our state-of-nature myths could change the way we think about the behavior of states in the international system. The use of the Hobbesian analogy in international relations theory is based on a partial view of human nature that is stereotypically masculine; a more inclusive perspective would see human nature as both conflictual and cooperative, containing elements of social reproduction and interdependence as well as domination and separation. Generalizing from this more comprehensive view of human nature, a feminist perspective would assume that the potential for international community also exists and that an atomistic, conflictual view of the international system is only a partial representation of reality. Liberal individualism, the instrumental rationality of the marketplace, and the defector's self-help approach in Rousseau's stag hunt are all, in analagous ways, based on a partial masculine model of human behavior.[92]

These characterizations of human behavior, with their atomistic view of human society, do not assume the need for interdependence and cooperation.[93] Yet states frequently exhibit aspects of cooperative behavior when they engage in diplomatic negotiations. As Cynthia Enloe states, diplomacy runs smoothly when there is trust and confidence between officials representing governments with conflicting interests. She suggests that many agreements are negotiated informally in the residences of ambassadors where the presence of diplomatic wives creates an atmosphere in which trust can best be cultivated.[94] As Enloe concludes, women, often in positions that are unremunerated or undervalued, remain vital to creating and maintaining trust between men in a hostile world.

Given the interdependent nature of contemporary security threats, new thinking on security has already assumed that autonomy and self-help, as models for state behavior in the international system, must be rethought and redefined. Many feminists would agree with this, but given their assumption that interdependence is as much a human characteristic as autonomy, they would question whether autonomy is even desirable.[95] Autonomy is associated with masculinity just as femininity is associated with interdependence: in her discussion of the birth of modern science in the seventeenth century, Evelyn Keller links the rise of what she terms a masculine science with a striving for objectivity, autonomy, and control.[96] Perhaps not coincidentally, the seventeenth century also witnessed the rise of the modern state system. Since this period, autonomy and separation, importantly associated with the meaning of sovereignty, have determined our conception of the national interest. Betty Reardon argues that this association of autonomy with the national interest tends to blind us to the realities of interdependence in the present world situation.[97] Feminist perspectives would thus assume that striving for attachment is also part of human nature, which, while it has been suppressed by both modern scientific thinking and the practices of the Western state system, can be reclaimed and revalued in the future.

Evelyn Keller argues for a form of knowledge that she calls "dynamic objectivity . . . that grants to the world around us its independent integrity, but does so in a way that remains cognizant of, indeed relies on, our connectivity with that world."[98] Keller's view of dynamic objectivity contains parallels with what Sandra Harding calls an African worldview.[99] Harding tells us that the Western liberal notion of instrumentally rational economic man, similar to the notion of rational political man upon which realism has based its theoretical investigations, does not make sense in the African worldview where the individual is seen as part of the social order and as acting within that order rather than upon it. Harding believes that this view of human behavior has much in common with a feminist perspective; such a view of human behavior could help us to begin to think from a more global perspective that appreciates cultural diversity but at the same time recognizes a growing interdependence that makes anachronistic the exclusionary thinking fostered by the state system.

Besides a reconsideration of autonomy, feminist theories also offer us a different definition of power that could be useful for thinking about the achievement of the type of positive-sum security that the women at The Hague and in Halifax and Nairobi described as desirable. Hannah Arendt, frequently cited by feminists writing about power, defines power as the human ability to act in concert or action that is taken with others who share similar concerns.[100] This definition of power is similar to that of psychologist David McClelland's portrayal of female power which he describes as shared rather than assertive.[101] Jane Jaquette argues that, since women have had less access to the instruments of coercion (the way power is usually used in international relations), women have more often used persuasion as a way of gaining power through coalition building.[102] These writers are conceptualizing power as mutual enablement rather than domination. While not denying that the way power is frequently used in international relations comes closer to a coercive mode, thinking about power in these terms is helpful for devising the cooperative solutions necessary for solving the security threats identified in the Halifax women's definitions of security.

These different views of human behavior as models for the international behavior of states point us in the direction of an appreciation of the "other" as a subject whose views are as legitimate as our own, a way of thinking that has been sadly lacking as states go about providing for their own security. Using feminist perspectives that are based on the experiences and behavior of women, I have constructed some models of human behavior that avoid hierarchical dichotomization and that value ambiguity and difference; these alternative models could stand us in good stead as we seek to construct a less gendered vision of global security.

Feminist perspectives on national security take us beyond realism's statist representations. They allow us to see that the realist view of national security is constructed out of a masculinized discourse that, while it is only a partial view of reality, is taken as universal. Women's definitions of security are multilevel and multidimensional. Women have defined security as the absence of violence whether it be military, economic, or sexual. Not until the hierarchical social relations, including gender relations, that have been hidden by realism's frequently depersonalized discourse are brought to light can we begin to construct a language of national security that speaks out of the multiple experiences of both women and men. As I have argued, feminist theory sees all these types of violence as interrelated. I shall turn next to the economic dimension of this multidimensional perspective on security.

3

Three Models of Man: Gendered Perspectives on Global Economic Security

The servant role of women is critical for the expansion of consumption in the modern economy.
—J. K. GALBRAITH

Economic development, that magic formula, devised sincerely to move poor nations out of poverty, has become women's worst enemy.
—DEVAKI JAIN

The majority [of women] still lag far behind men in power, wealth and opportunity.
JAVIER PEREZ DE CUELLAR

Since their birth in seventeenth-century Europe, states have engaged in political practices designed to promote their economic security. Trade and immigration barriers have been erected at national boundaries to protect domestic industry and domestic workers. Huge economic inequalities in the world are sustained through the protection of these state boundaries. Mercantilism, the leading school of economic theory in seventeenth- and eighteenth-century Europe, prescribed state intervention to promote economic self-sufficiency and favorable trade balances as a way of assuring na-

An earlier version of this chapter appeared in Murphy and Tooze, eds., *The New International Political Economy.*

67

tions' wealth, power, and military potential. With the establishment of economic liberalism as the leading school of economic theory in the nineteenth century, however, national growth and wealth were seen as fostered by freer modes of investment, migration, and exchange.

In the nineteenth century, politics and economics became separate academic disciplines. This separation, encouraged by the strong anti-Marxism of liberal economics, was an important influence on twentieth-century Western international relations scholarship, which largely neglected economic relations between states until the 1970s. When economic issues surfaced, they were relegated to matters of "low politics" as the "high politics" of national security and war took precedence.

In the 1970s, however, international political economy emerged as a more central topic of concern in mainstream Western international relations scholarship. The fact that economic relations were central to international politics, as well as the political implications of states' international economic behavior, could no longer be ignored. After thirty years of nuclear stalemate, military relations between the great powers were frozen; relations between advanced capitalist states, who were also partners in the Western alliance and therefore unlikely military adversaries, were defined primarily in economic terms.

The end of the post–World War II era of fixed exchange rates and international monetary management in the early 1970s, the erosion of the dollar as the key currency in the international monetary order, which signaled the relative decline in the power of the United States in the world economy, and the rise of states such as Germany and Japan, whose power depended on economic rather than military might, caused renewed interest in political economy among scholars studying advanced capitalist states. A global recession that, it was believed, was connected to the rise in the price of oil in the early 1970s, and the demands for a New International Economic Order (N.I.E.O.) by Third World states put relations between North and South more centrally on the agenda of international relations. Contemporary Marxist theories about the unequal allocation of wealth in a capitalist world economy began to be taken more seriously by certain Western international relations scholars.

At the same time, peace researchers began to question whether the economic security of the state, so important to seventeenth- and eighteenth-century mercantilists, was synonymous with the economic security of its citizens. In many parts of the Third World, the failure of development strategies to solve problems of poverty called for an examination of hierarchical political relations between North and South as well as the uneven distributive effects of the world capitalist economy. The legitimacy of states that failed to meet the basic material needs of their citizens began to be questioned. In many states, military budgets and arms purchases were taking priority over the economic welfare of individuals. The term *structural violence* was used to denote the economic insecurity of individuals whose life expectancy was reduced, not by the direct violence of war but by domestic and international structures of political and economic oppression. Peace researchers began to define security in terms of "positive peace," a peace that included economic security as well as physical safety.

Depending on their normative orientation and area of concern, contemporary scholars of international political economy have used different approaches to investigate these various concerns. These approaches fit broadly into what Robert Gilpin has described as the three constituting ideologies of international political economy: liberalism, economic nationalism, and Marxism.[1] Gilpin defines an ideology as a belief system that includes both scientific explanations and normative prescriptions. Since none of these approaches discusses gender, we must assume that their authors believe them to be gender neutral, meaning that they claim that the interaction between states and markets, as Gilpin defines political economy, can be understood without reference to gender distinctions. Feminists would disagree with this claim; as I argued in chapter 1, ignoring gender distinctions hides a set of social and economic relations characterized by inequality between men and women. In order to understand how these unequal relationships affect the workings of the world economy—and their consequences for both women and men—models of international political economy that make gender relations explicit must be constructed.

This chapter will analyze these three ideologies or models in order to see whether they are indeed gender neutral with respect both to their scientific explanations and to their normative prescriptions. The individual, the state, and class—the central units of analysis for each of these models, respectively—will be examined to see whether they evidence a masculine bias in the way they are described and in the interests they represent. If this is the case, then it is legitimate to ask whether and how gender has circumscribed each model's understanding of the workings of the world economy; if a masculine bias is apparent in these representations, we must ask whether the normative preferences and policy prescriptions of each of these perspectives will promote the economic security of men more than women.

Having critiqued each model from the perspective of gender, I shall offer some feminist perspectives on international political economy. Just as women have been absent from the field of international relations, the few feminists who write about economics claim that their discipline has rendered women completely invisible. The field of economics has shown little interest in household production and volunteer work, or in women's particular problems and accomplishments in a market economy.[2] A growing literature on women and development has been marginalized from mainstream theories of political and economic development. Since very little literature on women and international political economy exists, once again I shall be drawing on feminist literature from other disciplines and approaches. Common themes in these various feminist approaches suggest that feminist perspectives on international political economy would start with assumptions about the individual, the state, and class that are very different from those at the foundation of Gilpin's three ideologies.

Liberalism

Economic liberalism, while it has distanced itself from political issues, has served as the foundation for the dominant approach to Western international political economy in the twentieth century. Its beginnings as a school of thought are associated with the work of Adam Smith whose *Wealth of Nations*, published in 1776, first promoted the idea of the efficiency of the market in the allocation of goods and services and the division of labor as the best way of increasing productivity and wealth. Critical of mercantilism, which supported government involvement in the economy, liberals believe that politics and economics should be separated. Goods and services are best distributed through the price mechanism and the laws of supply and demand, free from government interference. Smith's arguments about the benefits of the division of labor were carried into the international sphere by nineteenth-century British economist David Ricardo, who claimed that countries could best promote their economic welfare by specializing in goods they could produce most cheaply or "efficiently" and trading them on the international market. Liberals believe not only that free trade will result in the maximization of global wealth and human welfare but also that it will lead to peace and cooperation between states.

Although its proponents present it as a scientific theory with universal and timeless applications, liberalism has generally been the approach preferred by scholars and policymakers from rich and powerful capitalist states. Just as Britain was committed to economic liberalism during its period of hegemony in the nineteenth century, the United States was the strongest proponent of liberalism in the post–World

War II era during its period of political and economic supremacy.

Liberal theory takes the individual as the basic unit of analysis: according to liberals, human beings are by nature economic animals driven by rational self-interest. "Rational economic man" is assumed to be motivated by the laws of profit maximization. He is highly individualistic, pursuing his own economic goals in the market without any social obligation to the community of which he is a part.[3] Liberals believe that even though this instrumentally rational market behavior is driven by selfish profit motives, it produces outcomes that are efficient or beneficial for everyone—though they acknowledge that not everyone will benefit to the same extent. Economic security is best assured by economic growth, the benefits of which will trickle down and increase the income of the entire population. The detrimental effects of economic growth and market behavior, such as dwindling resources and environmental damage, are generally not considered.

Feminist Critiques of Liberalism

Feminist critiques of liberalism should begin with an examination of "rational economic man," a construct that, while it extrapolates from roles and behaviors associated with certain Western men and assumes characteristics that correspond to the definition of hegemonic masculinity discussed in chapter 1, has been used by liberal economists to represent the behavior of humanity as a whole. Nancy Hartsock suggests that rational economic man, appearing coincidentally with the birth of modern capitalism, is a social construct based on the reduction of a variety of human passions to a desire for economic gain.[4] Its claim to universality across time and culture must therefore be questioned. For example, Sandra Harding's African worldview, discussed in chapter 2, in which the economic behavior of individuals is embedded within a social order, is a communal orientation seen as "deviant" by neoclassical economic theory; yet it is one that represents a different type of economic behavior specific to other cultures. As Harding claims, it also contains some striking parallels with the worldview of many Western women.[5]

Hartsock and Harding are thus claiming that the highly individualistic, competitive market behavior of rational economic man could not necessarily be assumed as a norm if women's experiences, or the experiences of individuals in noncapitalist societies, were taken as the prototype for human behavior. Women in their reproductive and maternal roles do not conform to the behavior of instrumental rationality. Much of women's work in the provision of basic needs takes place outside the market, in households or in the subsistence sector of Third World economies. Moreover, when women enter the market economy, they are disproportionately represented in the caring professions as teachers, nurses, or social workers, vocations that are more likely to be chosen on the basis of the values and expectations that are often emphasized in female socialization rather than on the basis of profit maximization. If this is the case, we must conclude that many women's, as well as some men's, motivations and behavior cannot be explained using a model of instrumental rationality; rather, these behaviors call for models based on different understandings of the meaning of rationality.

Rational economic man is extrapolated from assumptions about human nature that originate in British liberal political theory of the seventeenth and eighteenth centuries. Rational economic man bears many similarities to Hobbesian man, whose aggressive passions have been tamed by the rational pursuit of profit. Liberal contract theories about individuals' origins, such as that of Hobbes's, depict a state of nature where individuals exist prior to and apart from the community; they come together, not out of any desire for community, but out of the need for a protected environment in which they can conduct their economic transactions more securely without the threat of physical violence. Hartsock argues that, given its dependence solely on economic exchange, any notion of community in liberal theory is fragile and instrumental. She claims, however, that this liberal assumption, that the behavior of individuals can be explained apart from society, is unrealistic since individuals have always been a part of society.[6]

Although early liberal theorists were explicit in their assertion that their models of human behavior applied to men, not women, this distinction has since been lost, because contemporary liberals assume that humanity as a whole behaves in the same way. Feminist critics take issue with this theory of human behavior, asserting that it is biased toward a masculine representation. Harding claims that, for women, the self is defined through relationship with others rather than apart from others.[7] Alison Jaggar argues that liberalism's individualistic portrayal of human nature has placed excessive value on the mind at the expense of the body. In our sexual division of labor, men have dominated the intellectual fields while women have been assigned the "domestic" tasks necessary for physical survival; Jaggar concludes that, given this traditional sexual division of labor, women would be unlikely either to develop a theory of human nature that ignored human interdependence or to formulate a conception of rationality that stressed individual autonomy. If the need for interdependence were taken as the starting point, community and cooperation would not be seen as puzzling and problematic when we begin to think about alternative ways to define rationality.[8]

Generalizing from rational economic man to the world economy, liberals believe that world welfare is maximized by allowing market forces to operate unimpeded and goods and investment to flow as freely as possible across state boundaries according to the laws of comparative advantage. Critics of liberalism question this belief in openness and interdependence, claiming that it falsely depoliticizes exchange relationships and masks hidden power structures. They challenge the notion of mutual gains from exchange by focusing on the unequal distribution of gains across states, classes, and factors of production, and argue that in fact gains accrue disproportionately to the most powerful states or economic actors. For example, critics of liberalism would argue that liberal economic theory obscures the unequal power relations between capital and labor: since capital is mobile across interstate boundaries and controls strategic decisions about investment and production, it is being rewarded disproportionately to labor, a trend that was on the rise in the 1980s when labor was becoming increasingly marginalized in matters of economic policy.[9]

If capital is being rewarded disproportionately to labor in the world economy, then men are being rewarded disproportionately to women. A 1981 report to the U.N. Committee on the Status of Women avers that while women represent half the global population and one-third of the paid labor force and are responsible for two-thirds of all working hours, they receive only one-tenth of world income and own less that 1 percent of world property.[10] While much of women's work is performed outside the formal economy, these data suggest that women are not being rewarded to the same extent as men even when they enter the market economy. Although no systematic data on men's and women's incomes on a worldwide scale exists, an International Labor Office study of manufacturing industries in twenty countries, conducted in the mid-1980s, showed that women's wages were less than men's in each case.[11] Earning lower wages and owning an insignificant proportion of the world's capital puts women at an enormous disadvantage in terms of power and wealth and thus contributes to their economic insecurity.

While feminist economists are just beginning to explore the differential effects of the operation of the market economy on men and women, one area where these effects have been examined in some detail is in studies of Third World women and development.[12] Liberal modernization theory, a body of literature that grew out of assumptions that free markets and private investment could best promote economic growth in the Third World, saw women's relative "backwardness" as the irrational persistence of traditional attitudes. For example, the United Nations' Decade for the Advancement of Women (1975–85) assumed that women's problems in the Third World were related to insufficient participation in the process of modernization and development. In 1970, however, Esther Boserup, the first of many women scholars to challenge this assumption, claimed that in many parts of the colonial and postcolonial world, the position of rural women actually declined when they became assimilated into the global market economy.[13] Women's marginalization was exacerbated by the spread of Western capitalism and culture. In the preindependence period, Western colonizers rarely had any sympathy for the methods women used to cultivate crops; assuming that men would be more efficient as agricultural producers, they attempted to replace women's cultivation practices with those of men.

Boserup and others claim that development aid in the postcolonial period has actually reduced the status of women relative to men. After World War II, Western development experts taught new techniques for the improvement of agriculture to men who were able to generate income from cash crops. When land enters the market, land tenure often passes into the hands of men. Hence women's access to land and technology actually often decreases as land reform is instituted and agriculture is modernized. Land reform, traditionally thought to be a vital prerequisite for raising agricultural productivity, frequently reduces women's control over traditional use rights and gives titles to male heads of households. During the early years of development assistance, the concept of male head of household was incorporated into foreign assistance programs; according to the traditional Western sexual division of labor, imposed on societies with quite different social norms, women were seen as child rearers and homemakers, thus further marginalizing their productive activities.

The mechanization of agriculture in the Third World has also reduced women's control over agricultural production as men have taken over the mechanized part of the production process. The modernization of agriculture, which often leads to a dualism in agricultural production, tends to leave women behind in the traditional sector.[14] But in spite of mechanization, which remains largely in the hands of men, women continue to produce more than half the world's food: in sub-Saharan Africa, women are responsible for more than 80 percent of agricultural production. While women make up the majority of subsistence farmers, their activities have become less socially valued as cash cropping increases. Women's agricultural knowledge has generally been considered "unscientific" and therefore neglected in development programs.[15] Development experts talk to men, even when projects being designed may be more relevant for women's productive activities.[16]

While agriculture became more central to development planning in the 1970s, early Western liberal development strategies focused on industrialization, claiming that the economic growth it generated would trickle down to all sectors of the economy. As women were channeled into low-paying activities in industrial sectors of the Third World, the urban division of labor along gender lines became even more hierarchical than in subsistence agriculture. Since women are rarely trained as skilled industrial workers, the skills gap in many urban areas has increased, with women taking up domestic service or unskilled factory jobs. States that have adopted successful export-oriented industrial policies, such as South Korea, Taiwan, and Hong Kong, have relied to a considerable extent on unskilled women workers. Certain states have attracted overseas corporations by offering a large pool of docile young female laborers; these young women are frequently fired when they marry, try to unionize, or claim other benefits.[17] Cynthia Enloe claims that as long as young women working in "Export Processing Zones" are encouraged to see themselves as daughters or prospective

77

wives earning pin money rather than as workers their labor will be cheapened and women will have little opportunity to move into more skilled positions.[18]

Liberals, believing in the benefits of free trade, have generally supported export-led strategies of development. But since states that have opted for export-led strategies have often experienced increased inequalities in income, and since women are disproportionately clustered at the bottom of the economic scale, such strategies may have a particularly negative effect on women. The harsh effects of structural adjustment policies imposed by the International Monetary Fund on Third World debtor nations fall disproportionately on women as providers of basic needs, as social welfare programs in areas of health, nutrition, and housing are cut. When government subsidies or funds are no longer available, women in their role as unpaid homemakers and care providers must often take over the provision of these basic welfare needs.[19] Harsh economic conditions in the 1980s saw an increased number of Third World women going overseas as domestic servants and remitting their earnings to families they left behind.

These feminist studies of Third World development and its effects on women are suggesting that liberal strategies to promote economic growth and improve world welfare that rely on market forces and free trade may have a differential impact on men and women. Since women's work often takes place outside the market economy, a model based on instrumentally rational market behavior does not capture all the economic activities of women. Therefore we cannot assume that the prescriptions generated by such a model will be as beneficial to women's economic security as they are to men's.

Economic Nationalism

The intellectual roots of the contemporary nationalist approach to international political economy date back to the mercantilist school of sixteenth-, seventeenth-, and eighteenth-century Europe, the period that coincided with the rise of the modern state. The contemporary version of economic nationalism is quite similar to the realist school of international relations discussed in chapter 2 in terms of its assumptions about the international system and its explanations of the behavior of states. Just as liberalism is the ideology of rich and powerful states, economic nationalism became popular in the United States in the 1970s, at the same time its proponents became concerned with what they perceived as America's hegemonic decline.[20] The economic nationalist approach takes the state and its behavior in the international system as its basic unit of analysis. All economic nationalists subscribe to the primacy of the state, of national security, and of military power in the organization and functioning of the international system. While not denying that an open world economy could be mutually beneficial if all states adhered to liberal principles, economic nationalists, like realists, believe that states must act to protect their own economic interests lest they fall prey to others' self-seeking behavior in a conflictual international system lacking any international governance.

While contemporary economic nationalism became popular in the United States as a critique of the impracticality of liberal strategies in an illiberal world, its explanations for the behavior of states are quite similar to liberals' explanations of the behavior of rational economic man. States are assumed to be behaving as instrumentally rational profit maximizers, pursuing wealth, power, and autonomy in an international system devoid of any sense of community. In a conflictual world, states are striving to be economically self-sufficient. Their participation in the world economy is an attempt to create an international division of labor and resource allocation favorable to their own interests and those of groups within their national boundaries. Arguments against extensive economic interdependence are justified in the name of national security. Strategic domestic industries are to be given protection especially when they produce military-related goods. National security and national interest are thus the overriding goals of policy.[21] Like their seventeenth-century mercantilist predecessors, contemporary economic nationalists believe that, where necessary, the workings of the market must be subordinated to the interests of the state.

Feminist Critiques of Economic Nationalism

Feminist critiques of the economic nationalist approach should begin by examining the state, the central unit of analysis. If, as I argued in the previous chapter, the state is a gendered construct with respect both to its historical origins and to its contemporary manifestations, we might assume that prescriptions for maximizing state power could work to promote the economic welfare of men more than women.

The consolidation of the modern state system and the rise of modern science, from which the Western social sciences trace their origins, both occurred in the seventeenth century—a time of dramatic social, economic, and political upheaval well documented in Western history. Less well documented is the fact that the seventeenth century was also associated with the intellectual origins of Western feminism. According to Juliet Mitchell, this is not coincidental; women in the seventeenth century saw themselves as a distinct sociological group completely excluded from the new society that was rising out of the medieval order. She cites seventeenth-century feminists such as Mary Astell, who lamented that the new spirit of equality did not apply to women.[22]

Economic historians have similarly celebrated the rise of a new economic order, the beginnings of the drive to modernization and a market system that was to generate the unprecedented wealth of modern capitalism. But at such moments of great historical change usually identified with progress, feminist historians claim that women are often left behind economically or even made worse off. Just as Third World women have been marginalized through the infusion of Western gender roles into non-Western cultures, concepts of

gender and the gender linking of productive roles were shifting in the seventeenth century in ways that were marginalizing women's labor in Europe itself. In the seventeenth
century, definitions of male and female were becoming polarized in ways that were suited to the growing division
between work and home required by early capitalism but not
necessarily to the interests of women. The notion of "housewife" began to place women's work in the private domestic
sphere as opposed to the public world of the market inhabited by rational economic man. According to R. W. Connell,
the notion of the "home" did not exist in Europe before the
eighteenth century. As a combination of technology and industrial politics gradually pushed women out of core industries during the Industrial Revolution, gendered concepts of
the "breadwinner" and the "housewife" were constructed,
concepts that have been central to the modern Western definition of masculinity, femininity, and modern capitalism.[23]
The concept of housewife has continued to allow for the
provision of women's labor as a free resource until the present day.

While these new economic arrangements were synonymous with the birth of the Enlightenment, femaleness became associated with what Enlightenment knowledge had
left behind. The persecution of witches, who were defending
female crafts and medical skills of a precapitalist era against
a growing male professionalism, reached new heights in the
sixteenth and seventeenth centuries. Jean Bodin (1530–96), a
French mercantilist and founder of the quantitative theory of
money as well as the modern concept of national sovereignty, was one of the most vocal proponents of the persecution of witches. According to Bodin's mercantilist philosophy, the modern state must be invested with absolute sovereignty for the development of new wealth necessary for
fighting wars; to this end the state needed more workers and
thus must eliminate witches who were held responsible for
abortion and other forms of birth control.[24]

Sovereignty and rationality were part of an Enlightenment

epistemology committed to the discovery of universal objective or "scientific" laws, an epistemology that also discredited superstitions often portrayed as "old wives tales."[25] As discussed earlier, notions such as objectivity and rationality, central to the definition of the modern natural and social sciences in the West, have typically been associated with masculine thinking. According to Evelyn Fox Keller, Western cultural values have simultaneously elevated what is defined as scientific and what is defined as masculine.[26] In her study of the origins of modern science in the seventeenth century, Keller claims that modern scientific thought is associated with masculinity. Keller bases her claim on psychological theories of gender development, which argue that the separation of subject from object is an important stage of childhood "masculine" gender development. As infants begin to relate to the world around them, they learn to recognize the world outside as independent of themselves. Since an important aspect of this development of autonomy is separation from the mother, it is a separation that is likely to be made more completely by boys than by girls.

Whereas the Greeks had relegated the economy largely to the world of women and slaves, in seventeenth-century Europe the economy was elevated to the public domain of rational scientific knowledge, a domain composed mostly of men. The economic nationalist approach has taken the liberal concept of rational economic man, which grew out of this Enlightenment knowledge, and used it to explain the behavior of states in the international system. Using game theoretic models, such explanations of states' behavior draw on the instrumentally rational market behavior of individuals. Since international economic interactions rarely result in winner-take-all situations, economic nationalists have focused on Prisoner's Dilemma games, similar to those used by neorealists to explain the strategic security dilemma, to explain states' economic behavior in the international system. Where international economic cooperation is seen to exist, it is explained not in terms of international community but rather in terms of enlightened self-interest in an environment that is essentially anarchic.[27]

In her feminist critique of game theory, Birgit Brock-Utne cites recent research to support her claim that men and women exhibit different types of behavior when playing Prisoner's Dilemma games. Challenging a research finding that suggests that men may be more cooperative than women since, in single-sex Prisoner's Dilemma games, men choose a cooperative strategy more often than women, Brock-Utne claims that this is because men are more interested than women in strategic considerations of winning the game. When given a choice, men prefer games of skill, while women prefer games of chance. Since Prisoner's Dilemma is a game of skill, this may explain why women tend to lose interest when playing such games and fail to figure out the best strategy to maximize gains.[28] If, as Brock-Utne suggests, women tend to find this type of game based on instrumental rational behavior uninteresting, it is unlikely that they would have selected this methodology for explaining the behavior of states in the international economic system.

Using game theoretic models to explain states' behavior in the international system, economic nationalists, like the neorealists discussed in chapter 2, often portray states as unitary actors; concentrating at the interstate level, economic nationalists do not generally focus their attention on the internal distribution of gains. But if, as I have argued, women have been peripheral to the institutions of state power and are less economically rewarded than men, the validity of the unitary actor assumption must be examined from the perspective of gender. We must question whether women are gaining equally to men from economic nationalist prescriptions to pursue wealth and power. In all states, women tend to be clustered at the bottom of the socioeconomic scale; in the United States in the 1980s, 78 percent of all people living in poverty were women or children under eighteen.[29] In the United States, certain feminists have noted a trend toward what they term the increasing feminization of poverty: in the 1970s and 1980s,

THREE MODELS OF MAN

families maintained by women alone increased from 36 percent to 51.5 percent of all poor families.[30] In societies where military spending is high, women are often the first to feel the effects of economic hardship when social welfare programs are sacrificed for military priorities. As I have mentioned before, for economic nationalists the military-industrial complex is an important part of the domestic economy entitled to special protection. For poor women, however, the trade-off between military and economic spending can pose a security threat as real as external military threats.

I have shown that the economic nationalist explanation of states' behavior in the international system, which focuses on instrumental rationality, is biased toward a masculine representation. Moreover, the evolution of the modern state system and the capitalist world economy changed traditional gender roles in ways that were not always beneficial to women. Contemporary economic nationalist prescriptions for maximizing wealth and power can have a particularly negative impact on women since women are often situated at the edge of the market or the bottom of the socioeconomic scale.

Marxism

Contemporary Marxist approaches to international political economy come out of the perspective of the weak and powerless on the peripheries of the world economy. Like economic nationalism, contemporary Marxist approaches also arose as a critique of liberalism; unlike economic nationalists, however, Marxists deny that economic openness, even if it were adhered to by all states, could ever result in mutually beneficial gains. Writers in the dependency and world systems schools, not all of whom are Marxists but all of whom owe an intellectual debt to Marxism, argue that the capitalist world economy operates, through trade and investment, in a way that distorts the economies of underdeveloped states in the Third World and condemns them to permanent marginalization; their participation in the world capitalist economy is seen as detrimental to their development and as exacerbating both domestic and international inequalities between the rich and the poor.[31] Concepts of core and periphery, which exist both in the world economy and within the domestic economies of states themselves, are used to explain these inequalities: class alliances between capitalists in the Third World and transnational capital contribute to the further marginalization of peripheral sectors of Third World economies.[32] Therefore, according to these writers, both the domestic and international political and economic relations of Third World capitalist states are embedded in the exploitative structures of a capitalist world economy. Authentic, autonomous development, which meets the economic security needs of all people, can be achieved only by a socialist revolution and by the very difficult task of breaking detrimental ties with the world economy.

Feminist Critiques of Marxism

Since they speak for the interests of the least powerful in the international system, Marxist theories would appear to be more compatible with feminist perspectives. In fact much of recent feminist theory owes a strong intellectual debt to Marxism. Like Marxists, radical, socialist, and postmodern feminists see knowledge as historically and socially constructed. Marxists and feminists would agree that knowledge is embedded in human activity. Like much of feminist theory, many Marxists reject both the notion of a universal and abstract rationality and the claims of "objectivity" upon which both the liberal and economic nationalist approaches to international political economy depend so heavily.

For feminists, the Marxist understanding of knowledge is helpful because it supports their claim that knowledge has been constructed in such a way that it denies a voice to women. Nevertheless, feminism is often critical of Marxism; feminists who claim to be Marxists acknowledge that Marxist theory is in need of considerable revision if it is to speak to the various interests of women. Feminists criticize Marxist theories for ignoring women in their reproductive and domestic roles and for assuming that class-based capitalist oppression is synonymous with women's oppression.

Contemporary Marxist approaches to international political economy take class as their basic unit of analysis. In classical Marxist theory, women were subsumed under this class analysis rather than discussed as a group with particular interests and needs. In *The Origin of the Family, Private Property, and the State*, Frederick Engels tied women's oppression to male ownership of private property under capitalism and to women's dependence on men for their subsistence. Engels and other Marxists believed that when women entered the labor market, they would be made economically independent and could join with working-class men in the overthrow of capitalism, thus leading to liberation for both men and women under socialism.[33]

Socialist feminists argue that this type of class-based analysis ignores two important factors: first, that women are oppressed in specific ways that are attributable to patriarchy rather than to capitalism; and, second, that class analysis ignores women's role in the family. These feminists maintain that women do not have the same opportunities as men when they enter the work force in any society, socialist or capitalist. As discussed earlier, women worldwide earn less than men on an average, even when performing similar tasks. The problem of child care hinders women's entry into the job market and when they do enter the labor market women tend to be ghettoized in low-paying jobs or to face wage discrimination. In all societies, jobs that are predominantly occupied by women are considered less prestigious and therefore less well paid than those occupied by men. Women frequently experience harassment and intimidation in the workplace, and taking time off to bear and raise children may threaten job security and impede opportunities for promotion.

However, it is Marxism's tendency to ignore women in

their reproductive roles that feminists criticize the most. For classical Marxists, procreation was seen as a natural female process, fixed by human biology. Therefore a division of labor, whereby women are primarily responsible for the rearing of children, was also seen as relatively fixed.[34] Since it assumed that women's role as caretakers of children was "natural," an assumption now questioned by many feminists, classical Marxism omitted women's roles in the family from its analysis. Feminists argue that ignoring women in their reproductive and child-rearing roles, an omission common to all approaches to political economy, leaves all the unpaid labor that women perform in the family outside of economic analysis.[35] By ignoring women in their domestic roles, Marxists and non-Marxists alike neglect certain issues that are peculiar to women, regardless of their class position. When married women move into the labor force they usually continue to be responsible for most of the housework and child rearing.[36] Besides the lack of respect for unpaid housework and the dependence of full-time housewives on the incomes of their husbands, women, including those in the work force, usually suffer a severe decline in income should their marriage end in divorce. Economic dependence may force women to stay in violent and abusive marriages.

Gender ideologies, which dictate that women should be mothers and housewives, justify discriminatory practices in the labor market and place a double work burden on women. Maria Mies suggests that the historical process of the development of the gendered role of housewife in early modern Europe was an important part of the evolution of the capitalist world economy. She argues that the "nonproductive" labor of women was the foundation upon which the process of capital accumulation got started on a global scale. Mies claims that the processes of imperialism and "housewifization" were causally interrelated in nineteenth-century Europe: housewifization encouraged the demand for luxury items produced in the colonies to be consumed by European women, thus moving the display of luxury from the public to the private domain. Housewifization also produced the Victorian image of the good woman withdrawn from war, politics, and money-making, with the consequence that women's labor became a natural resource that was freely available outside the wage economy. Mies ties all these historical practices to the workings of the contemporary global economy in which former colonies are still producing consumer goods for the First World, production often undertaken by poorly paid women whose low wages are justified as supplementary income for future mothers and housewives.[37]

If Marxist theories have paid insufficient attention to the historical evolution of women's private roles in households, feminist writers also claim that contemporary Marxist analysis, which focuses on the structural problems of Third World economies, does not deal adequately with the position of marginalized women in these areas. Although they often play a crucial role in subsistence production, women in the Third World are increasingly being defined as dependents, which further reinforces their marginality and denies them access to the monetary economy.[38] While dependency theory claims that the continued marginalization of those in the subsistence sector is a structural consequence of the dualisms produced by capitalist development, it does not acknowledge the disproportionate numbers of women among the marginalized, nor the fact that the status of women relative to men has been declining in many parts of the Third World.

Studies based on the contemporary situation in Europe and North America suggest that women make up a slight majority of the world's population; when women have similar nutritional standards and get similar medical treatment to men, they tend to live longer. On a global scale, however, women do not constitute a majority of the population. Mies argues that there has been a steady decline in numbers of women in proportion to men in India since the beginning of the twentieth century. She attributes this to a higher mortality rate of female babies and young girls as well as to a high maternal mortality rate. In instances where overall mortality rates have been reduced, studies show that women receive less adequate health treatment and have lower nutritional standards than men.[39]

As reported in the *New York Times* of June 17, 1991, data from China's 1990 census reveal that 5 percent of infant girls born in China are unaccounted for. In a society where boys are strongly preferred, China's one-child-per-couple population policy may result in girls not being registered at birth or being put up for adoption. While infanticide is considered to be rare, ultrasonic testing to determine the sex of the fetus allows for the abortion of females, a practice that is increasing in many parts of the Third World.

Amartya Sen reveals that population studies in the Third World in general suggest that more than 100 million women are missing, a statistic that speaks of the inequality and neglect that leads to the excessive mortality of women. Economic development is quite often accompanied by a relative worsening of the rate of women's survival resulting from the fact that women do not share equally in the advances in medical and social progress. Calling it one of the "more momentous and neglected problems facing the world today," Sen asserts that, in view of the enormity of this problem, it is surprising that this issue has received so little attention.[40] Feminists would be less surprised than Sen; claiming that the negative effects of the world economy on women have been ignored by all schools of international political economy, they would say that the particular oppression of women evident in such data must be explained by gender-discriminating practices that include, but extend well beyond, the effects of capitalism.

If, as many feminists claim, women's oppression is due to patriarchy as well as capitalism, could the position of women be expected to improve under socialism, as Marxists believe? Socialist feminists agree that the condition of women in socialist states usually improves in the areas of social policies, welfare, and legal rights.[41] The availability of maternity rights, day care, and other institutional reforms may further improve the position of working women in socialist states. However, studies of women in the Soviet Union in the 1980s found that while women constituted 51 percent of the work force, they were disproportionately concentrated in unskilled jobs and continued to carry most of the domestic workload.[42] Although traditional Marxism saw women's entry into the labor force as a liberation, women in the former Soviet Union have seen it as an additional burden on top of demanding household duties in a state that chose to sacrifice consumer interests to state-centric heavy industrialization.[43]

Since interference in the family as an institution is as much resisted in socialist states as it is in capitalist states, problems of powerlessness and violence, which women encounter in families, remain. Moreover, writers on women in socialist states generally conclude that, even if women's conditions in the work force are improved, women are as poorly represented in positions of state power and decision making as they are in capitalist states. These feminists argue that, although women may suffer from particular forms of repression under capitalism, the liberation of women through class struggle cannot be assumed. It will only come about when women are equal to men in both the public and the private spheres, a condition that would not necessarily obtain in a postcapitalist world.

Feminist Perspectives on International Political Economy

I have shown that the individual, the state, and class, which are the basic units of analysis for the liberal, economic nationalist, and Marxist approaches to international political economy, respectively, are biased toward masculine representations. Hence the prescriptions that each of these models offers for maximizing economic welfare and security may work to the advantage of men more than women. I shall now discuss how we might go about constructing feminist perspectives upon which to build less gender-biased representations of international political economy, perspectives that would include the various economic security needs of women.

The liberal and economic nationalist perspectives both rely on an instrumental, depersonalized definition of rationality that equates the rationality of individuals and states with a type of behavior that maximizes self-interest. These approaches assume that rational action can be defined objectively, regardless of time and place. Since most nonliberal feminists assume that the self is in part constructed out of one's place in a particular society, they would take issue with this definition of rationality: agreeing with Marxists, they would argue that individuals and states are socially constituted and that what counts as rational action is embodied within a particular society. Since rationality is associated with profit maximization in capitalist societies, the accepted definition of rationality has been constructed out of activities related to the public sphere of the market and thus distinguished from the private sphere of the household. Feminists argue that, since it is men who have primarily occupied this public sphere, rationality as we understand it is tied to a masculine type of reasoning that is abstract and conceptual. Many women, whose lived experiences have been more closely bound to the private sphere of care giving and child rearing, would define rationality as contextual and personal rather than as abstract. In their care-giving roles women are engaged in activities associated with serving others, activities that are rational from the perspective of reproduction rather than production.

A feminist redefinition of rationality might therefore include an ethic of care and responsibility. Such a definition would be compatible with behavior more typical of many women's lived experiences and would allow us to assume rational behavior that is embedded in social activities not necessarily tied to profit maximization. It could be extended beyond the household to include responsibility for the earth and its resources, a concern that is quite rational from the perspective of the survival and security of future generations.

Liberal, economic nationalist, and Marxist perspectives have all tended to focus their analysis at the systems level, whether it be the international system of states or the world capitalist economy. Feminist perspectives on political economy should be constructed from the bottom up, from the standpoint of those at the periphery of the world economy or the international system. Feminist perspectives should take the individual as the basic unit of analysis, but an individual defined differently from rational economic man. Since feminists claim that the liberal assumption of individual autonomy and self-sufficiency is unrealistic, feminist perspectives would assume a connected, interdependent individual whose behavior includes activities related to reproduction as well as production. In order to capture these productive and reproductive activities, the artificial boundaries between the world of instrumentally rational economic man in the public sphere of production and the socially rational activities that women perform outside the economy as mothers, care givers, and producers of basic needs must be broken down. Destroying these barriers would help to reduce the differential value attached to the "rational" or "efficient" world of production and the private world of reproduction. Were childbearing and child rearing seen as more valued activities, also rational from the perspective of reproduction, it could help to reduce the excessive focus on the efficiency of an ever-expanding production of commodities, a focus whose utility in a world of shrinking resources, vast inequalities, and increasing environmental damage is becoming questionable. A perspective that takes this redefined individual as its basic unit of analysis could help to create an alternative model of political economy that respects human relationships as well as their relation to nature.[44]

This feminist redefinition of rationality allows us to take

as a starting point the assumption that the economic behavior of individuals is embedded in relationships that extend beyond the market. Maria Mies argues that the production of life should be defined as work rather than as unconscious natural activity. Labor must include life-producing work and subsistence production rather than being restricted to surplus-producing labor. Instead of accepting the sexual division of labor as natural, feminist perspectives should place the production of life as the main goal of human activity and work toward breaking down the artificial division of labor created along gender lines that perpetuates the devaluation of women's work.[45]

To make women's work valued by society, the barriers between public and private must be broken down. Subsistence labor, volunteer work, household work, and reproduction are among the economic activities performed primarily by women that are not counted as economically productive. Marilyn Waring claims that women have been rendered invisible in national accounting data. Since these kinds of women's work are not included in the annual reports of the International Monetary Fund, the World Bank, or the development agencies, projects are not planned with women in mind. While economists have claimed that nonmonetary labor is too hard to count, Waring suggests some ways, such as time-use data, which would make this possible.[46]

If a substantial portion of women's productive and reproductive activities are taking place on the peripheries of the world economy in households or in the subsistence sector of Third World economies, feminist perspectives must be concerned with achieving economic justice in these particular contexts. While agreeing that women's domestic labor should be recognized as work, feminists caution that economic security for women in households cannot be guaranteed in the family as it is presently constituted. Although the family has been designated as the private sphere of women, the concept of male head of household has ensured that male power has traditionally been exercised in the private as well as the public realm. Susan Okin argues that families are not just to women or children as long as women continue to bear a disproportionate share of child rearing, have lower expected incomes than men, and are left with primary responsibility for supporting and caring for children if families break up. Okin claims that only when paid and unpaid work associated with both productive and reproductive labor is shared equally by men and women can the family be a just institution and one that can provide the basis for a just society.[47]

As I have already discussed, Third World development strategies have tended to ignore the subsistence sector where much of women's labor is being performed, with the result that modernization has had a differential impact on men and women and has in certain instances actually reduced the position of women. Due to the virtual absence of women from local and national power structures, development programs have tended to support projects in areas of production that are dominated by men. To achieve economic justice for rural women in the Third World, development must target projects that benefit women, particularly those in the subsistence sector. Improvements in agriculture should focus on consumption as well as production; in many parts of Africa, gathering water and fuel, under conditions of increasing scarcity and environmental degradation, are taking up larger portions of women's time and energy.

Since women are so centrally involved in the satisfaction of basic needs in households and in the subsistence economy, feminist approaches to international political economy must be supportive of a basic needs approach where basic needs are defined inclusively, in terms of both material needs and the need for political participation. I have argued that export-oriented development strategies have tended to contribute to domestic inequality and, in times of recession and increasing international indebtedness, have had a particularly detrimental impact on women; a strategy that seeks to satisfy basic needs within the domestic economy may thus be the best type of strategy to improve the welfare of women.

Local satisfaction of basic needs requires more attention to subsistence or domestic food production rather than to growing crops for export markets. A more self-reliant economy would also be less vulnerable to the decisions of foreign investors, whose employment policies can be particularly exploitative of women.[48] Basic needs strategies are compatible with values of nurturance and caring; such strategies are dependency-reducing and can empower women to take charge of their own lives and create conditions that increase their own security.

As Anne Marie Goetz claims, women have been completely absent from the process of setting national development priorities. I argued previously that women must be seen as agents in the provision of their own physical security; creating conditions under which women become agents in the provision of their own economic security is also imperative. Just as women are seen as victims in need of protection in the protector/protected relationship, when women become visible in the world economy, they tend to do so as welfare problems or as individuals marginalized from mainstream development projects. Separating women from men, often as an undifferentiated category, ignores the importance of relations between men and women and the detrimental effects of hierarchical gender relationships on women's economic security. It also ignores the ways in which women's varying identities and development interests as farmers, factory workers, merchants, and householders bear on gender relations in different contexts.[49] To overcome the problems of essentialization as well as the perception of victimization, women must be represented at all levels of economic planning, and their knowledge must be seen as valuable rather than unscientific.

At a time when existing political and economic institutions seem increasingly incapable of solving many global problems, feminist perspectives, by going beyond an investigation of market relations, state behavior, and capitalism, could help us to understand how the global economy affects those on the fringes of the market, the state, or in households as we attempt to build a more secure world where inequalities based on gender and other forms of discrimination are eliminated. Looking at the world economy from the perspective of those on its fringes can help us think about constructing a model concerned with the production of life rather than the production of things and wealth. Maria Mies argues that the different conception of labor upon which such a model depends could help us adapt our life-style at a time when we are becoming increasingly conscious of the finiteness of the earth and its resources.[50]

I shall now turn to a consideration of conditions necessary for the security of our natural environment and to an examination of how feminist perspectives could also help us to think about the achievement of ecological security.

4
Man over Nature: Gendered Perspectives on Ecological Security

Taking care of one planet is nothing special, nothing
sacred, nothing holy. It's something like taking care
of our own house.
—DALAI LAMA

Americans did not fight and win the wars of the
20th century to make the world safe for
green vegetables.
—RICHARD DARMAN

Until very recently ecological concerns have not been at the center of the agenda of international relations theory or practice. A global issue that defies national boundaries and calls for collective action, caring for the environment does not fit well with the power-seeking, instrumental behavior of states that I have described in previous chapters. Barry Commoner's definition of ecology as the "science of planetary housekeeping"[1] is not the business of Realpolitik; such metaphors evoke images of the devalued private domain of women rather than the "important" public world of diplomacy and national security. Ecological bumper stickers with such messages as "Love Your Mother" are hardly designed to appeal to those engaged in the "serious" business of statecraft and war. Therefore the inattention to environmental problems and the silencing of women in international relations may be more than coincidental.

The term *ecology*, which means the study of life forms "at home," is based on the Greek root for house; its modern meaning is the interrelationships between living organisms and their environment.[2] These definitions evoke images of a domestic space traditionally populated by women, children, and servants. Ecology's emphasis on holism and reproduction and metaphors such as global housekeeping connect it to women's rather than men's life experiences.

Yet ecology has also been viewed with some ambivalence by feminists. Many of them are suspicious of ecology and ecofeminism because they regard the age-old connection between women and nature, which both have espoused, as a basis of women's oppression. Socialist feminists, particularly, have criticized what they see as ecofeminists' tendency to essentialize women and naturalize their reproductive and domestic roles. This tendency perpetuates the dualistic hierarchies described in chapter 1 that most feminists believe must be eliminated if gender equality is to be achieved.[3] Yet some recent ecofeminist scholarship is rejecting this essentialist connection between women and nature, as well as making important and interesting alliances with the ecological tradition. Believing that the oppression of women and the domination of nature are both the result of patriarchy, these ecofeminists claim that the connection must be made explicit if structures of domination in both our natural and human environments are to be overcome. For this reason, these feminist ecological perspectives can offer us important new insights into the way we think about our natural environment, insights that could be useful for thinking about the achievement of global ecological security.

Since its birth in seventeenth-century Europe, the modern state system has had an uneasy relationship with its natural environment; natural resources and geographical spaces have been viewed as resources for increasing state power and wealth. Feminist writers such as Carolyn Merchant and Evelyn Fox Keller describe a fundamental change in the Western scientific community's attitude toward the natural environ- ment that also began in seventeenth-century Europe. Before this scientific revolution, nature had been seen as a living system of which humans formed an integral part; in the seventeenth century, human beings became preeminent, and nature began to be viewed as a machine to be exploited for human benefit. This mechanistic view of nature has been highly compatible with the needs of a competitive interna- tional system, a world divided into antagonistic political units, each seeking to enhance its power by securing and increas- ing access to natural resources, through geographical expan- sion when necessary.

Since this is a worldview that has had important, although often implicit, implications for the evolution of the theory and practice of international relations, I shall begin this chap- ter with a feminist account of the way nature has been viewed by Western Enlightenment science. This changed perception of nature, from living organism to inert machine, was accom- panied by shifting attitudes toward women whose lives were gradually being moved into domestic spaces where they were to become increasingly marginalized from the productive system. These changes can be linked to the competitive se- curity-seeking behavior of an expansionary state system, whose colonizing activities have caused ecological changes in larger geopolitical spaces. This power-seeking behavior poses dangers for the security of the natural environment and its inhabitants, women and men alike.

Although raising environmental issues only marginally, scholars in conventional international relations approaches have assumed that natural resources are an important ele- ment of state power and thus vital for national security. Recently, however, some new thinking in international rela- tions has begun to question these assumptions; the pressure on what is now seen as a finite resource base, as well as the inability of states to deal with environmental degradation, is threatening the security of all, whether rich or poor. These new thinkers also draw attention to international inequalities associated with environmental degradation and attempt to revisualize geopolitical spaces and boundaries from an ecological perspective.

Although much of this new thinking questions the optimistic assumptions of Enlightenment science about nature's rejuvenative ability to provide unlimited resources for human progress, it remains firmly rooted in an Enlightenment view of nature as machine. Only ecologists and ecofeminists have taken an even more radical step, one that challenges modern science's mechanistic view of nature. I shall conclude this chapter by examining the views of ecologists and ecofeminists who believe that solutions to our contemporary dilemmas demand a revolution, not only in our political thinking but also in the way we view nature—in other words, a revolution as fundamental as the one that took place in seventeenth-century Europe.

The Modern State and Its Natural Environment

Hans Morgenthau's text *Politics Among Nations*, discussed in more detail in chapter 2, pays scant attention to the natural environment, an omission common to many traditional texts in international relations. Morgenthau discusses natural resources only in terms of their role as essential elements of state power.[4] He emphasizes the importance of natural resource self-sufficiency as crucial for national power, particularly in wartime. He describes dramatic historical shifts, such as the disappearance of the Near East and North Africa as centers of power, caused by a notable decline in agricultural productivity. Consistent with the Western geopolitical tradition of the early twentieth century, Morgenthau claims that the United States owes its status as a great power in part to its advantageous geographical position in the international system. As a large land mass protected by bodies of water on both sides, the United States has been in a strategically advantageous position throughout the latter half of the twentieth century, particularly for purposes of making credible nuclear threats.

Morgenthau's treatment of natural resources and geopolitics typifies the way the natural environment has been viewed in the dominant traditions of Western international relations theory. In a hierarchical international system, access to natural resources and a favorable geographical position have been key elements for the achievement of state power; for those with the capabilities to do so, these assets should be protected by military means and increased through overseas expansion or conquest if necessary.[5]

State-of-nature myths, used by realist theoreticians to explain and prescribe for states' behavior in the international system, have reinforced this dominating and exploitative attitude toward nature. Metaphors that depict a wild natural environment devoid of controlling political institutions, "the war of everyman against everyman," demand the erection of strong boundaries to protect tamed domestic spaces against uncontrollable outside forces. States with the capacity to do so may move beyond these boundaries to reap the bounties of nature through projects of expansion and subjugation.

Nature, Women, and the State in Early Modern Europe

These views of the natural environment as spaces to be tamed, mastered, and used for profit and advantage are also reflected in the shift toward a mechanistic view of nature that appeared in seventeenth-century Europe at the time the modern state system was born. In her book *The Death of Nature*, Carolyn Merchant documents this changing attitude toward nature generated by the scientific revolution. Although humans' "dominion over nature" has been traced back to Greek and Christian roots,[6] Merchant claims that in medieval Europe nature was viewed as an organism or living system in which human beings and their natural environments were highly interdependent. Nature was generally depicted as female, the earth as a nurturing mother who provided for the needs of humankind. Nature could be dangerous, however; its wild and uncontrollable behavior could produce chaos.[7] In the seventeenth century nature was gradually conceptually transformed from a living organism into a lifeless inert machine, thereby permitting its exploitation and use for purposes of human progress. This evolving view of nature as machine was vital for the goals of the emerging new science, which sought to tame nature through the discovery of predictable regularities within a rationally determined system of laws. According to Merchant, a central concern of the scientific revolution was to use these mathematical laws in order to intervene in an increasingly secularized world.[8]

Changing attitudes toward animals provide further evidence of the taming and depersonalization of nature in early modern Europe. In her book *The Animal Estate,* Harriet Ritvo describes the legal system of medieval England, which had implicitly invested animals with human rights and responsibilities. Animals were held accountable for their crimes: dogs, cats, and cocks were permitted, as members of households, to testify in court—or at least their presence there was considered to strengthen the aggrieved householder's complaint.[9] By the nineteenth century, however, animals could no longer be sentenced to die for their crimes. Ritvo claims that this seemingly humanitarian policy had a reverse side; animals were no longer perceived as having any independent status. This changing relationship between animals and people ensured the appropriation of power by people as animals became objects of human manipulation. As animals' position in the human world changed so did the way in which they were studied. According to Ritvo, modern scientific methods of classification of animals and plants, which employ anthropocentric binary distinctions such as wild/tame, useful/useless, edible/inedible, also attempt to impose order on a chaotic natural environment. Just as many feminists see gender dichotomizations as instruments of domination, Ritvo views the classification of natural objects as the human attempt to gain intellectual mastery and domination of the natural world.[10]

Although Ritvo's study is not specifically a feminist text, she makes reference to language employed by naturalists and animal breeders that sets both women and animals below human males in the natural hierarchy.[11] The use of sexual metaphor, which feminists believe had the effect of establishing a male-dominated hierarchy, was also employed in the language of the scientific revolution. The taming of nature was usually described in gendered terms that reflected the social order. Feminist scholars have drawn attention to the sexual metaphors employed by Francis Bacon and other Enlightenment scientists. Central to Bacon's scientific investigations was a natural world, frequently described as a woman, that required taming, shaping, and subduing by the scientific mind: "I am come in very truth leading you to nature with all her children to bind her to your service and make her your slave."[12] Social ecologist William Leiss agrees that Bacon's scientific project was centrally concerned with mastery over nature. But while Leiss notes the sexually aggressive overtones in Bacon's language, he is less concerned with the implications of Bacon's sexual metaphors than with a scientific tradition that has resulted in the domination of certain men over other human beings. This system of domination has spread outward from Europe to the rest of the world through the appropriation of nature's resources.[13]

Feminist scholars such as Carolyn Merchant, Sandra Harding, and Evelyn Fox Keller, who have written about the origins of modern science, would agree with Leiss's argument that domination of nature was a central goal of modern science. Using a gendered perspective, however, they take his argument further: suggesting that the sexual imagery in seventeenth-century science was intrinsic to its discourse, they claim that the domination of certain men over other human beings, other cultures, and nature cannot be fully understood unless this gendered language is taken seriously.

In her discussion of metaphors in science, Sandra Harding

asks why certain metaphors, such as the rape of nature, have been dismissed by historians and philosophers as irrelevant to the real meaning of scientific concepts while others, such as the metaphor of nature as a machine, have been regarded as fruitful components of scientific explanation.[14] Harding and Keller claim that these gendered metaphors are crucial for understanding Western science as a masculine enterprise. The separation of mind from nature and the investigator from his or her subject of investigation have been important goals for modern science's quest for objectivity. But as reason was separated from feeling and objectivity from subjectivity, science came to be defined in opposition to everything female. This kind of knowledge is consistent with a project that has involved the mastery, control, and domination of nature.[15] These feminists therefore believe that such seventeenth-century gendered metaphors were fundamental to developing attitudes toward nature and women, as well as the racist attitudes toward non-Western peoples that I described; these attitudes have been consistent with the practices of an expansive and dominating international system.

As seventeenth-century science associated nature and the body with women, so the mind, or rational thought, came to be associated with men. In the West, culture has generally been linked historically and symbolically with elite men whose writings, music, and art are enshrined as the canons of Western civilization. According to Merchant, this nature/culture dichotomy was used as a justification for devaluing women and keeping them in subordinate positions in early modern Europe. As documented by Merchant, Keller, and other feminist scholars, the Enlightenment was not a progressive time for women; as is often the case in eras that have traditionally been described as progressive, the position of women in public life suffered a setback in the seventeenth century. Women's association with a disorderly nature was personified by an increase in the persecution of witches, who were linked to the superstition and chaos that modern science was attempting to control and tame through its investigations. Both Merchant and Leiss note the legal metaphors in Bacon's language, metaphors that Merchant explicitly links to seventeenth-century witch trials.[16] Simultaneously, the needs of early industrial capitalism stimulated a growing division of labor between home and workplace that began the process of severely curtailing the economic, political, and social options available to women.[17]

This transition to a capitalist market economy required a greater exploitation of natural resources than did the subsistence economy of feudal Europe. Merchant outlines changes in seventeenth-century English agriculture, which began to encroach on woods and fen lands in the pursuit of the higher yields required for production for the market. Seventeenth-century scientists justified their goals of "mastering" and "managing" the earth in the name of human progress and increasing material wealth. The demands of a market economy, and the increases in productivity that it generated, required the use of nonrenewable energy resources such as timber and coal. Rendering nature as a dead, inert object was essential for eliminating fears that the mining of metals and fuels crucial for the coming industrial revolution was a violation of nature's inner resources.

The Domination of Nature Globalized

A nascent market economy and its need for an ever-expanding resource base, together with a new vision of scientific progress, were important motivating forces as the early modern state system began to expand beyond its European boundaries. Europeans started venturing overseas in search of additional wealth and natural resources. Merchant describes an ecological crisis—caused by Europe's shipbuilding industry, an industry that was one of the most critical for subsequent commercial expansion and national supremacy—that occurred as early as the sixteenth century. Shipbuilding, which depended on mature oaks for masts and hulls, created a severe wood shortage in many parts of Europe, forcing the turn to mining coal as an alternate source of fuel.[18] As Europeans began to sail beyond their shores, the exploitation of natural resources in the name of human progress took on wider dimensions, beginning a process that has culminated in the twentieth century's highly interdependent global resource base with its strong potential for increasing international competition and conflict over scarce resources. As ecological crises have begun to take on global dimensions, humanity's vision of conquering nature has even extended beyond the earth into space. Schemes for mining the moon and using the material to create a "Pittsburgh in space" are being envisaged.[19]

In an international system consisting of autonomous sovereign political units, the notion of the world as a single resource base has led inevitably to political competition and conflict. European expansion and imperialism extended the seventeenth century's instrumental view of nature beyond the boundaries of Europe as scientific progress became in itself a justification for imperialist projects. The Enlightenment belief that the transformation of the environment was a measure of human progress was used as a justification for colonialism, because native populations were not deemed capable of effecting this transformation for themselves.[20] Thus the lower position assigned to women and nature in early modern Europe was extended to members of other cultures and races.

Harriet Ritvo argues that the growing dichotomy between domestic and wild animals in modern Europe was frequently compared to the dichotomy between civilized and savage human societies; she cites a report, to which Charles Darwin refers in his writings, of two Scottish collies who visited Siberia and "soon took the same superior standing" with regard to the native dogs "as the European claims for himself in relation to the savage."[21] The Regents Park Zoo, opened in London in 1828, was a celebration of England's imperial enterprise; wild animals from all over the world were displayed as evidence of England's ability to subdue exotic territories and convert their wild products into useful purposes. Ritvo cites a popular nineteenth-century zoology text that compares the ferocity of wild animals to the barbarity of native populations: when describing Africa, its author claims that "in all countries where men are most barbarous, the animals are most cruel and fierce."[22]

Carolyn Merchant asserts that by 1700 "nature, women, blacks and wage laborers were set on a path toward a new status as 'natural' and human resources for the modern world system."[23] "Empty" or "virgin" lands became sites for European conquest and settlement; according to Vandana Shiva, *wastelands*, a word loaded with the biases of colonial rule, were seen as spaces to be cultivated for the generation of revenue and resources for the "mother" country.[24] In reality, these spaces were not empty at all but occupied by people with very different relationships with their natural environment. The expansion of the European state system meant that the scientific revolution and its mechanistic attitude toward nature began to take on global dimensions with far-reaching implications for non-Western ecological traditions, most of which have been lost to the cultural imperialism of the West.

Merchant's account of changing attitudes toward nature in seventeenth- and eighteenth-century New England provides a case study of one such ecological revolution caused by European expansion.[25] Before European colonization, Native American populations, living in subsistence communities, regarded natural resources as gifts given by nature to take care of human needs; humans and animals lived in interlacing, cyclical time and space. As European settlers moved into these spaces they saw these new lands very differently, as "wastes" or wildernesses to be tamed and "improved," projects that required the expertise of a "superior" culture. The scientist Robert Boyle, who was also the governor of the New England Company, declared his intention of ridding the "Indians" of their "ridiculous" notions

about the workings of nature whom they misguidedly perceived "as a kind of goddess."[26] This taming process gradually set humans, European and native alike, apart from nature. Although Native Americans continued to be associated
with animals in the minds of European settlers, and were
thus placed below Europeans in the social and political hierarchy, Native Americans began to see themselves as distanced from natural resources and apart from nature. Through
their involvement in the fur trade Native Americans began
to objectify nature as it became associated with commercial
transactions, and the killing of animals was undertaken for
profit rather than survival.[27]

Merchant's account of the next phase of this ecological
revolution in early New England parallels her earlier work
on seventeenth-century Europe. As agricultural production
was transformed from subsistence to market, farming gradually changed into a manufacturing industry. As this transformation took place, production and reproduction were split
into separate spheres, and women became defined by their
reproductive function within the private sphere. Commercial
farming, conducted mostly by men, required the management of nature as an abstract mechanical force; nature as
mother retreated into the private sphere along with women,
who were expected to be the upholders of moral values that
had no place in a market economy.[28]

Merchant's conclusion is an ironic one when framed in a
global perspective. She argues that since contemporary New
England depends on outside sources for most of its energy,
food, and clothing some of its own environment has re-
covered, as evidenced by the regeneration of its natural forests. However, we should remember that today it is people
in the Third World who are suffering the gravest consequences of resource depletion: with its colonial legacy as
supplier of raw materials to the "civilized" world, the Third
World today suffers some of the harshest effects of environmental degradation. The demands upon the world's resources by the Eurocentric state system have imposed and

continue to impose heavy burdens on the natural environment and its human inhabitants worldwide.

Nature and the Reconceptualization of Geographic Space

The mechanistic attitude toward nature that began in seventeenth-century Europe and was subsequently globalized through imperialism led to a fundamental shift in the conceptualization of geographical space. Merchant notes that in the case of early America a breakdown of the Native American way of life began with the mapping of their homeland onto geometric space by European explorers and mapmakers. As space was reorganized, fixed boundaries between wild and civilized appeared, boundaries unknown to Native American cultures. The mapping of the world by European explorers led to similar processes of reconceptualizing and organizing geographical space on a global scale, a process that has lent itself to projects of management, control, and domination of the environment.

The history of spatial changes is also the history of power changes.[29] The interrelation between geographical space and power politics noted by Hans Morgenthau and other contemporary international relations scholars was developed more comprehensively by the Western geopolitical tradition of the nineteenth and early twentieth centuries. Although it fell from favor in Western international relations scholarship in the post–World War II period, owing to its association with Nazism, geopolitical thinking had considerable influence on United States containment policies of the Cold War era.[30]

In his study of Western geopolitical thought, Geoffrey Parker defines geopolitics as the study of international relations from a spatial viewpoint; geopolitics views the world as an interlocking mechanism, an assumption that links it to the Enlightenment view of nature as a machine.[31] While looking at the globe as a totality, geopolitics sees a world divided into bounded political entities competing for control over their environment. Citing Friedrich Ratzel's description of the state as an organism engaged in a competitive struggle of evolution and decay, Parker notes the Darwinian influence on nineteenth-century geopolitical thinking.[32] The German school of Geopolitik, of which Ratzel was a member, was founded on environmental determinism: the power that any state could command depended on its geographical circumstances. In geopolitical terms, spaces are contested areas populated by colonists, soldiers, navies, and traders. As geopolitical thinkers along with mapmakers were effecting this transformation in our perception of the global environment, the native inhabitants of these spaces were being marginalized, just as women were increasingly being confined to the private space of the family.

By the end of the nineteenth century, the expansion of the European state system had brought the entire world into an integrated space upon which the geopolitical tradition imposed the hierarchical notion of order and power that has been fundamental to traditional international relations theory and practice. While geopolitics made explicit the domination that states have attempted to impose on their natural environment, modern science's mechanistic view of nature provided the framing assumptions basic to the Western tradition of international relations theory. Hobbes's *Leviathan*, his solution to the dangers inherent in this system, is a mechanistic model of society in which order can be guaranteed only by an absolute sovereign operating the machine from outside.[33] The lack of such a sovereign in the state of nature leads to disorder, which results from unbridled competition for scarce resources. As discussed in a previous chapter, this condition of "anarchy" has been used by realists as a metaphor to portray the international system; the wildness of nature beyond the boundaries of an orderly "domesticated" political space demands that states try to control and dominate this external environment through the accumulation of national power that can protect their attempts to appropriate necessary natural resources.

Hobbes's *Leviathan* was a model for a society developed in

the seventeenth century when the perception of the universe shifted from organic to mechanistic. According to Merchant, one of the most significant achievements of mechanism as a worldview was its reordering of reality around a masculinist notion of order and power.[34] In addition to their potential for dominating nature, machines brought certainty and control. In international relations, the search for control has also led theorists and practitioners to mechanistic models such as power balancing with its seeming promise of imposing order on a disorderly international system. But power balancing and its resultant practice of self-help through military means if necessary do not offer solutions for the security of the natural environment. Paradoxically, the quest for national security, which involves the appropriation of natural resources through the domination of global space, is a historical process that has actually contributed to a decline in the security of the natural environment. Given the potential of modern weapons for mass destruction, military force, the last resort of states for security enhancement, has become the ultimate threat to the natural environment.

This paradox has stimulated some international relations scholars to begin reconceptualizing security in ecological terms and to challenge the traditional formulations of geographical space. Such thinking attempts to move beyond a worldview whose boundaries are imposed by traditional national security concerns to one that reconceptualizes geographical space in terms of the fragility of the natural environment and its human inhabitants.

From National Security to Environmental Security

From Geopolitical to Ecopolitical Space

The erection of boundaries has been an important part of the modernist goal to tame nature and impose order and control on dangerous geographical spaces. The geopolitical tradition has drawn our attention to boundaries and spaces carved out by states to enhance their security and command over natural resources. New thinking on environmental security first drew attention to environmental degradation by eliminating these boundaries altogether. Pictures of earth, sent back from the Apollo II spacecraft in 1969, were used to change our spatial perception of the globe from a world divided into hierarchical, competitive states to "spaceship earth," a fragile, interconnected whole whose inhabitants—women, men, and nonhuman forms of life—were equally at risk. "From space, we see a small and fragile ball dominated not by human activity and edifice but by a pattern of clouds, oceans, greenery, and soils."[35] This new image underscored the uselessness of state boundaries as protection against ecological threats. As Patricia Mische reminds us, the Great Wall of China, the only human creation visible from space, was built to protect against invaders, but it has now become victim to the forces of nature, dwarfed by mountains and other natural features and offering protection against nothing.[36]

Just as Merchant describes a reformulation of geopolitical space brought about by an ecological revolution in early New England, scholars concerned with environmental degradation today are challenging us to rethink once again our ideas about contemporary geopolitical space. In an era where modern ecological revolutions have had dramatic impacts on non-Western cultures and peoples worldwide, these new thinkers encourage us to look at the world not as a system of land-based states but as a global unit sharing a dependence upon one atmosphere and upon a single body of water that encompasses 70 percent of the earth's surface. Harold and Margaret Sprout visualize the world not according to familiar maps that depict national boundaries, but as an ecosystem, a global unity of natural carriers composed of the atmosphere and seawater.[37] Although they do not believe that the state is withering away, they do suggest that it is becoming unviable for the provision of personal safety and the survival of the human species.[38] While it is too early to speak of a world community in the political sense, the Sprouts see a tightening interdependence that is forging a community in an ecological sense.

This fragile ecosystem cannot be protected by boundaries, traditional instruments of national security. Problems of the ozone layer, acid rain, and river and ocean pollution are impervious to national boundaries. Just as nuclear testing in the South Pacific has posed severe dangers for local populations, no state in Western Europe was able to protect itself against radiation from the Chernobyl nuclear accident in Ukraine in 1986. The hole in the ozone layer over Antarctica, which is suspected of causing a rise in skin cancer in Australia, is thought to be the result of pollution emanating primarily from the Northern Hemisphere. Military power, traditionally used by states to ensure protection of their boundaries from external threats, is seen by environmentalists as not only useless but counterproductive. While modern warfare inevitably imposes enormous devastation on the natural environment, as was evident in the war in the Persian Gulf in 1991, weapons testing, military maneuvers, and waste from weapons production contribute to environmental destruction even in peacetime. Military hardware is highly energy intensive. As military spending continues to increase in all parts of the world, environmentalists draw attention to the trade-offs between military and environmental spending. The Worldwatch Institute has estimated that expenditure of a cumulative sum of about $774 billion during the 1990s, a sum less than annual world military spending since the early 1980s, could turn around the adverse trends in soil erosion, deforestation, and decline in energy efficiency, as well as contribute to the development of renewable sources of energy.[39]

Global insecurities, as a result of these environmental threats and resource scarcities, were further underscored by the literature on global modeling that, in the early 1970s, began to produce dire warnings of physical "Limits to Growth." Emphasizing this one-world image, forecasts from the Club of Rome predicted that an exponential growth of population and industrially caused pollution would collide with a fixed environment sometime in the next fifty to one hundred years, causing dramatic population decreases and a decline in the quality of life due to a depletion of natural resources, a rise in pollution, and a shrinking of the food supply.[40] Its highly controversial conclusions suggested that only if population increases and economic growth were halted could catastrophe be avoided.

While these universalizing images of "one world" and its fragility have served to alert people to the dangers of environmental degradation and resource constraints, they have seriously depoliticized issues that remain embedded in the historical practices of the European state system. The image of "Mother Earth" tames and domesticates our perception of a world in which this historically expansive system has been responsible for the erection of contemporary boundaries between North and South, rich and poor, and men and women.[41] These boundaries of inequality affect the way in which environmental dangers influence people's lives. While the affluent are concerned with the potential hazards of a thinning ozone layer, the poor are confronted by more immediate environmental degradation, such as contaminated water and soil erosion, which threaten their daily existence.

The cleavage between North and South became apparent at the United Nations Conference on the Environment in 1972, when representatives from states in the South criticized the North for prioritizing the issue of environmental pollution. Although the South has softened its position on this issue somewhat, it continues to resent the attention given to pollution in international forums at the expense of its preferred definition of environmental problems in terms of poverty and maldistribution of resources. The South was highly critical of the Malthusian implications of the Limits to Growth literature that seemed to preclude any chance for a better life for the world's poor. Admonitions that economic growth must be stopped in all parts of the world, when an average person in an industrial market economy uses more than eighty times as much energy as someone in sub-Saharan Africa, were deemed unacceptable.[42] The South has also resented the North's concentration on population control in a world where resource use is highly unequal. Although documents such as *Our Common Future*, the 1987 report of the World Commission on Environment and Development, have tried to overcome the hostility engendered by the no-growth implications of the global modelers with calls for "sustainable development," a type of growth that respects environmental constraints,[43] the global effort to deal with the environment has continued to center on pollution, an issue of greater concern to states in the North.

Looking at environmental issues in terms of poverty, as the South demands, draws attention to boundaries that segregate the world's poor into areas of extreme environmental degradation and that render them immediate victims of environmental stress. In the South, disease from polluted drinking water is the single largest cause of premature death, young children being particularly at risk. The United Nations Environmental Program has estimated that 35 percent of the land surface of the earth is threatened with desertification.[44] Problems of desertification and soil erosion have caused widespread famine, particularly in the poorest countries where growing populations press upon inadequate land and fuel resources. In parts of the Sahel, refugees from environmental degradation face further hardships when they become involved in political and social problems such as tribal and ethnic disputes. These extreme problems are not limited to Africa. It has been estimated that one-sixth of the population of Haiti has left that country because of environmental degradation. Haiti suffers from some of the world's most severe soil erosion problems.[45]

Environmental boundaries that segregate the poor are generally the result of social or economic inequalities. For example, in Latin America in 1975, 7 percent of landowners possessed 93 percent of the most desirable land, while 83 percent of the population lived on plots too small to support a household, most of them either in damage-prone or forested land.[46] These immediate environmental insecurities are not limited to the rural poor or to people living in the South. Poor people living in urban slum conditions, in rich and poor countries alike, are also particularly vulnerable to environmental threats. In his discussion of "Black Ecology" Nathan Hare claims that blacks in the United States are concerned with the immediate problems of survival, overcrowding, work hazards, and infant mortality, rather than clean beaches and redwood trees.[47] Just as many African Americans are ghettoized in urban slums in the United States, other marginalized peoples are subject to arbitrary boundaries that wall off areas of environmental stress. Native Americans have been placed on some of the worst rural land in the United States, just as South African blacks have been relegated to overcrowded, resource-scarce townships.

For the most part, environmentalists who have described these particular insecurities of marginalized people have failed to address the particular plight of women, who are often the worst victims of environmental degradation. Even the Report of the World Commission on Environment and Development, an important internationally sponsored report on the environment, does not touch on the immeasurable consequences for women of the deterioration of the environment.[48] As gatherers of firewood and water, rural women in the Third World bear a large measure of responsibility for providing clean drinking water and energy for the household. Since they are responsible for household energy needs, women bear the burden of a severe fuelwood crisis that is widespread in many rural areas of the Third World. In rural areas throughout the world, women carry loads of wood weighing up to thirty-five kilograms as much as ten kilometers from home.[49] It is rarely pointed out that wood is being depleted more rapidly than any fossil fuel; since its consumers have little political power, it is not an issue that commands much attention from those concerned with environmental security. Environmental damage has a severe impact on women's reproductive systems; besides claiming the lives of thousands of victims, the accident at a pesticides plant in Bhopal, India, in 1984 had enormous repercussions for women who sought abortions for fear that the leakage of poison gas might cause birth defects. It was women who first organized the protest at Love Canal in New York State in the 1970s because of damage that began to show up in their own reproductive systems and in the bodies of their children. Mothers in toxically contaminated communities have become key environmental activists, often motivated by mothering an environmentally wounded child.[50]

The State and Environmental Security

A common theme running through much of the literature on international relations and environmental security is that the contemporary state system is not adequate for the task of solving these problems. Just as this system was born at a time of scientific revolution in the seventeenth century, many contemporary environmentalists believe that another revolution, the technological revolution of the late twentieth century, is creating problems with which this system of sovereign states will be unable to cope. Describing an international relations system in transition, Dennis Pirages claims that the state-centric, exclusionist paradigm described in chapter 2 no longer serves us well in dealing with the rapid changes being brought about by new technologies and their negative consequences.[51] Resource interdependence and pollution demonstrate the permeability of traditional international boundaries and the impossibility of separating domestic and international affairs. In a highly interdependent global ecosystem, many environmentalists believe that the contemporary state is becoming anachronistic.[52]

Traditional international relations theory, which describes the self-seeking, conflict-prone behavior of states and its detrimental effects on the natural environment, also offers a

pessimistic view of the potential of the state as an environmental manager of the global commons. As Rousseau's metaphor of the stag hunt suggests, collective action for the
common good is hard to achieve in anarchical realms with
no legally sanctioned method of enforcement. When public
goods such as clean air and water can be consumed by all
members of the system whether or not they pay for them,
states tend to act selfishly, hoping that others will bear the
costs. The Sprouts claim that when national governments
look to spaces outside their own territory, their concerns
reflect their own national values rather than the shared values of a global community.[53] Paradoxically, the great powers, the traditional managers of the international system,
pose the greatest threat to the environment by virtue of their
disproportionate consumption of resources, their high level
of pollution, and their possession of large numbers of environmentally threatening weapons. Given the principle of
state sovereignty, internal boundaries that contribute to environmental degradation are also hard to change when it is
not in the interests of national political and economic elites
to do so.

Consequently, many new thinkers on the environment
believe that environmental management must move either
up or down the organizational ladder but in any case away
from the state. The Report of the World Commission on
Environment and Development calls for a greater commitment on the part of international institutions and a greater
willingness of states to assign management responsibilities
to these global institutions. Others believe that global management will remove environmental issues from the democratic process and that care for the environment must start at
the local level with the involvement of individual women
and men. Many new thinkers believe that both domestic and
international bureaucratic institutions, as they are presently
organized around functionally specific tasks, are inadequate
for solving complex problems that require an interdisciplinary understanding of whole systems.

Many of these new thinkers submit that the international system, composed of states that have sought to ensure and enhance their own security at the expense of the natural environment and its individual inhabitants, requires a fundamental restructuring if it is to overcome our environmental dilemmas. Yet few of these scholars make similar inferences about the need to restructure the relationship between humans and nature that has evolved simultaneously with the globalization of the state system. Ecologists and ecofeminists offer this more radical challenge: only by changing our relationship with nature can real security, for both our natural environment and its human inhabitants, be achieved.

From Environmental Security to Ecological Security

While environmental managers, operating under short-term constraints, try to coax recalcitrant states into a more cooperative stance vis-à-vis environmental crises, ecologists, committed to a more radical reformulation of the way we view our natural environment, take a longer-term perspective. Ecologists believe that only with a fundamental revolution in the way in which we understand nature can problems of such magnitude be solved. The mechanistic view of nature, bequeathed to us by the scientific revolution of the seventeenth century, does not bode well for an ecologically secure future. But while calling for fundamental changes in both modern science and contemporary political, social, and economic structures as great as those set in motion in the seventeenth century, few ecologists have raised the issue of gender relations. Merchant and many other feminists, however, see this issue as fundamental to those social structures as well as to the projects of modern science. For this reason, ecofeminists would claim that the science of ecology cannot live up to its claim as a holistic science without including gender in its analysis. By making explicit the inherent connection between the domination of nature and the domination of women, ecofeminists claim that both must be overcome simultaneously if true ecological security is to be achieved.

An Ecological Perspective on Security

The science of ecology is interdisciplinary and multidimensional. It assumes that all living species are part of an ecosystem in which everything is interconnected: human beings are but one of many species making demands on the earth's resources. Ecologists claim that populations and their environments are related in ways that cause each to act on the other in dialectical fashion, just as the Native Americans in New England were themselves changed by the ecological revolution caused by European settlers. Ecology studies long-term trends in humans beings' relationship to their environment over the span of geological time. As was the case in premodern Europe, nature is still regarded as a mystery whose behavior must be observed and accepted rather than tamed and controlled.[54] Ecologists claim that only by understanding the complex functioning of living systems as wholes, and their interactions with their environment, can we hope to solve our contemporary ecological crises. This demands a methodology quite different from the atomized, reductionist methods of modern science, which, because it is not holistic, fails to see the harmful side effects of its activities. Ecologists' critiques of modern science parallel those made by feminists such as Merchant, Keller, and Harding.[55]

Like certain feminists, many ecologists are critical of modern society, given its dependence on an excessive appropriation of nature's resources. They suggest that the values of modern society are based on an incomplete model of humanity that emphasizes instrumental rationality, production, and consumption at the expense of humaneness, creativity, and compassion. "Economic man" is a compulsive producer and consumer, with little thought for ecological constraints. Modernization, which has legitimized these destructive behaviors, has led to a loss of control over science and technology that is causing severe environmental stress today.[56] Modernization, a product of the European Enlightenment, is now being reproduced in the Third World, where development projects often further strain limited environmental resources and reproduce inequality. Irene Dankelman and Joan Davidson claim that science's manipulations of nature, manifested in projects such as the Green Revolution, threaten the natural environment and marginalize poor people. As modern techniques are used to increase crop yields, water supplies begin to suffer from contamination from fertilizers and pesticides, making them less available for drinking. Modernization of agriculture in the Third World has encouraged monoculture and cash cropping, which makes women's tasks of feeding families more difficult. The authors point out that the ecological damage caused by modernization often falls most heavily on women in their role as family providers.[57]

Ecologists are critical of environmental management in general. They claim that management techniques grow out of the reductionist methodology of modern science that cannot cope with complex issues whose interdependencies are barely understood. Such methodologies, evident in the use of computer models, perpetuate the dominating, instrumental view of nature that attempts to render it more serviceable for human needs and that leaves hierarchies—feminists would include gender hierarchies—intact. A mechanistic view of nature leads to the assumption that it can be tinkered with and improved for human purposes, an assumption that is increasingly being questioned as negative consequences of projects such as high-yield agriculture are becoming more evident. Ecologists believe that only when knowledge is demystified and democratized, and not regarded as solely the possession of "experts," can an ecologically sound mode of existence be implemented.

As Patricia Mische points out, we have reached a point where just as the number of international agreements on the environment is increasing, so too is the level of environmental degradation. Mische claims that this is because agreements are usually reactive rather than anticipatory, selective rather than comprehensive.[58] If environmental management is barely able to keep pace with environmental degradation, ecologists believe that only with a fundamental change in human relationships with nature can we achieve real ecological security. As an alternative to "rational man," David Orr posits "ecological man," who would be less materialistic, his behavior more finely tuned to cycles of nature and to his own biological rhythms.[59]

In a similar vein, the Sprouts claim that a revolution in the way people view the world and their relation to it must take place in order to achieve environmental security. Human behavior is governed by both exploitative and mutualistic philosophies; to live in harmony with the natural environment, the Sprouts believe that it is necessary to move toward a greater reliance on mutualistic behavior, a type of behavior that they argue is more typical of family relations than public-sphere behavior.[60] Using the metaphor of the earth as an estate in trust to be prudently managed and bequeathed to posterity, the Sprouts universalize this ethic of care and responsibility associated with activities most often performed by women in the household. Although they are not explicit on this point, both Orr's construction of "ecological man" and the behavior recommended by the Sprouts are closer to most women's life experiences than to many men's.

An Ecofeminist Perspective on Security

Social ecologists such as William Leiss explicitly link man's domination of nature with certain men's domination over other human beings. Defending the original goals of the scientific revolution as an attempt to liberate human beings from the constraints of their natural environment and increase their material well-being, Leiss claims that the rationalism of modern science became caught in a web of social contradictions. The instruments through which human beings have transformed the resources of nature into means for the satisfaction of material desires have increasingly come to be regarded as objects of political conflict both domestically and internationally.[61] According to Leiss's class analysis, the real object of domination has not been nature but human beings: through enhanced technological capabilities certain people have appropriated nature's resources and thereby dominated others. A more rational science would understand the world in a way that would produce harmony with the environment. But this can be realized only when the struggle for domination ends, along with disparities in power among groups and nations.[62]

Social ecologist Murray Bookchin, one of the few ecologists who raises the issue of gender relations, also points to the hierarchical structuring of the contemporary world embodied in man's domination over man, woman, and nature. Bookchin believes that these modes of domination are historically constructed and can therefore be transcended. He stresses the emancipatory potential of ecology, a science that recognizes no hierarchy and is therefore in a position to combat domination at all levels.[63]

Bookchin claims that this Western hierarchical thinking, which valorizes male power, devalues women by associating them with its devalued image of nature. It is this essentialist connection between women and nature, made both by some ecologists and certain feminists, that contributes to many other feminists' reluctance to espouse an ecological perspective.[64] The immanent connection between women and nature, linked to women's biological functions, has been criticized by many feminists as demeaning, deterministically excluding women from the male domain of culture and transcendence. Yet recent work in feminist cultural anthropology disputes claims that this connection is innate and suggests instead that it is historically contingent: rooted in Western cultural traditions, it has been imposed on other cultures as part of the Western project of domination.[65]

If, as these anthropologists and social constructionist ecofeminists believe, Western civilization has reinforced the subjugation of women through its assertion that they are closer to nature than men, then the nature/culture dualism must be challenged rather than ignored. If, as these authors claim, the woman/nature connection is historically contingent, then there are possibilities for transcending this hierarchical dualism in ways that offer the promise of liberation for both women and nature. Since the liberation of nature is also the goal of ecology, ecofeminist Ynestra King suggests that feminism and ecology can usefully form an alliance. According to King, ecology is not necessarily feminist, but its beliefs are quite compatible with those of these social constructionist ecofeminists since both make their chief goal the radical undermining of hierarchical dualisms. King argues that, since ecofeminists believe that misogyny is at the root of the dualism between nature and culture that ecologists deplore, ecology is incomplete without feminism.[66]

While ecologists such as Leiss have connected the exploitation of nature to class domination, social constructionist ecofeminists make more explicit an interlocking pattern of dominance relationships that include sexism and racism as well as classism and that, they claim, are historically tied to the domination of nature. Joan Griscom believes that only when conceptual connections between all these forms of repressions are made can the emancipatory potential of ecology be fully realized.[67] According to ecofeminist Ynestra King, feminism challenges the male-based values of our culture: when coupled with an ecological perspective, it insists that all human beings, both women and men, remember and accept their origins in nature. King claims that ecofeminism is in a position to heal the splits in a world divided against itself and built on a fundamental lie: the defining of culture in opposition to nature. Only by seeking to overcome such hierarchical dualisms can we move toward a more harmonious relationship with our natural environment.[68]

Since women have been associated with a devalued nature through these hierarchical dualisms, women have a particular stake in ending the domination of nature. As I have stated, women are often the worst victims of environmental degradation. But just as I have argued against perceiving women as victims in the protector/protected discourse of national security, so women must not be seen solely as victims of environmental degradation but also as agents who must participate equally in the solution of these problems. Since women have not been well represented in national and international institutions dealing with the environment, their contribution to working for ecological security has been largely at the grassroots level. For example, the Chipko movement, which began with women hugging trees as a protest against cutting them down in the Chamoli district of Uttar Pradesh in 1973, met with some success when Indian prime minister Indira Gandhi issued a fifteen-year ban on the commercial felling of the forests of Uttar Pradesh. Women are also taking part in projects of reforestation; Kenya's Green Belt Movement, started in 1977 by the National Council of Women, involves women in the establishment of "Green Belt communities" and small tree nurseries.[69]

The kind of knowledge that women bring to these various environmental movements is gained from experience as producers and providers for daily household needs. However, the belief that this type of knowledge cannot be "scientific" has kept it from being recognized by development and environmental "experts" as well as foreign policymakers. As long as metaphors such as "global housekeeping" associate ecological security with the devalued realm of women, it will not become an issue of priority on the foreign policy agendas of states or in the mainstream discipline of international relations.

While it has paid little direct attention to environmental issues, the conventional discipline of international relations has relied to a great extent on modernity's mechanistic view of nature in framing its assumptions about the behavior of states in the international system. Feminist perspectives on ecology reveal not only the hierarchical relationship between humans and nature that has grown out of this worldview but also the extent to which this unequal relationship interacts with other forms of domination and subordination, including gender relations. The hierarchical dualisms discussed in this chapter, such as culture/nature, civilized/wild, North/South, rich/poor, public/private, and international/local, have been characteristic of the way in which we describe world politics and the interaction of states with their natural environment. A feminist perspective would argue that not until the boundaries of inequality and domination these dualisms represent are transcended can true ecological security be achieved. Only through the emergence of a system of values that simultaneously respects nature, women, and a diversity of cultures—norms that have been missing from the historical practices of international statecraft—can models that promise an ecologically secure future be devised.

5

Toward a Nongendered
Perspective on
Global Security

*If you dream about an egalitarian and just society
it cannot be created by men alone. You cannot
ignore 50% of the population.*
—SHEKHAR PATHAH

*It's terribly important, maybe even to the future of
the world, for women to take part in making the
decisions that shape our destiny.*
—JEANE KIRKPATRICK

*The woman most in need of liberation is the woman
within every man.*
—WILLIAM SLOANE COFFIN

In previous chapters I have argued that traditional notions of national security are becoming dysfunctional. The heavy emphasis on militarily defined security, common to the foreign policy practices of contemporary states and to the historical traditions from which these practices draw their inspiration, does not ensure, and sometimes may even decrease, the security of individuals, as well as that of their natural environments. Many forms of insecurity in the contemporary world affect the lives of individuals, including ethnic conflict, poverty, family violence, and environmental degradation; all these types of insecurity can be linked to the international system, yet their elimination has not been part of the way in which states have traditionally defined their national security goals.

Previous chapters have also called attention to the extent to which these various forms of military, economic, and ecological insecurity are connected with unequal gender relations. The relationship between protectors and protected depends on gender inequalities; a militarized version of security privileges masculine characteristics and elevates men to the status of first-class citizens by virtue of their role as providers of security. An analysis of economic insecurities suggests similar patterns of gender inequality in the world economy, patterns that result in a larger share of the world's wealth and the benefits of economic development accruing to men. The traditional association of women with nature, which places both in a subordinate position to men, reflects and provides support for the instrumental and exploitative attitude toward nature characteristic of the modern era, an attitude that contributes to current ecological insecurities.

This analysis has also suggested that attempts to alleviate these military, economic, and ecological insecurities cannot be completely successful until the hierarchical social relations, including gender relations, intrinsic to each of these domains are recognized and substantially altered. In other words, the achievement of peace, economic justice, and ecological sustainability is inseparable from overcoming social relations of domination and subordination; genuine security requires not only the absence of war but also the elimination of unjust social relations, including unequal gender relations.[1]

If, as I have argued, the world is insecure because of these multiple insecurities, then international relations, the discipline that analyzes international insecurity and prescribes measures for its alleviation, must be reformulated. The reconceptualization of security in multidimensional and multilevel terms is beginning to occur on the fringes of the discipline; a more comprehensive notion of security is being used by peace researchers, critics of conventional international relations theory, environmentalists, and even some policymakers. But while all these contemporary revisionists have helped to move the definition of security beyond its exclusively national security focus toward additional concerns for the security of the individual and the natural environment, they have rarely included gender as a category of analysis; nor have they acknowledged similar, earlier reformulations of security constructed by women.

Including previously hidden gender inequalities in the analysis of global insecurity allows us to see how so many of the insecurities affecting us all, women and men alike, are gendered in their historical origins, their conventional definitions, and their contemporary manifestations. Using gender as a category of analysis reveals the masculinist assumptions of both traditional and revisionist theories of international politics and economics. It also allows us to see the extent to which unequal gender relationships are a form of domination that contributes to many of the dimensions of the contemporary insecurities analyzed by various new thinkers. Feminists deny the separability of gendered insecurities from those describable in military, economic, and ecological terms; such problems cannot be fully resolved without also overcoming the domination and exploitation of women that takes place in each of these domains.

Such a conception of security is based on the assumption that social justice, including gender justice, is necessary for an enduring peace. While acknowledging that unequal social relations are not the only sources of insecurity, feminists believe that contemporary insecurities are doubly engendered. Beyond the view that all social institutions, including those of world politics, are made by human beings and are therefore changeable, they recognize that comprehensive security requires the removal of gender-linked insecurities. Revealing these gender inequalities allows us to see how their elimination would open up new possibilities for the alleviation of the various domains of global insecurity that I have described. Overcoming gender inequalities is necessary, not only for the security of women but also for the realization of a type of security that does not rely on characteristics associated with the hegemonic masculinity that has produced a kind of security that can be a threat to men's security also. Men are themselves insecure partly because of the exclusionary, gendered way their own security has been defined.

This final chapter will draw together some of the ways in which the integration of these gendered perspectives on international security can contribute to reformulating the discipline of international relations. However, the ultimate goal of such a reformulation must not be to replace the masculinist perspective on international relations that presently obtains with a feminist perspective. The integration of feminist perspectives into the discipline is but a necessary first step toward transcending gender as a category of analysis. The possibility of moving beyond these gendered perspectives would depend on redefining the discipline of international relations in such a way that women's experiences were included in its subject matter on an equal basis with men's. Such a transcendence can come about, however, only when oppressive gender hierarchies are eliminated.

What Do Gendered Perspectives on Global Security Tell Us About the Discipline of International Relations?

The gendered perspectives on security I have presented point to the conclusion that the discipline of international relations, as it is presently constructed, is defined in terms of everything that is not female. While classical realism has constructed its analysis out of the behavior and experiences of men, neorealism's commitment to a positivist methodology that attempts to impose standards of scientific inquiry used in the natural sciences, has resulted in an extreme depersonalization of the field that only serves to hide its masculinist underpinnings. My analyses of "political" and "economic" man, and the state as an international political and economic actor, all suggest that, beneath its claim to objectivity, realism has constructed an approach that builds on assumptions and explanations based on behaviors associated with masculinity. While many forms of masculinity and femininity exist that vary across class, race, culture, and history, international relations theories, and the world they analyze, privilege values associated with a socially constructed hegemonic masculinity. This hegemonic masculinity consists of a set of characteristics that, while they are drawn from certain behaviors of Western males, do not necessarily fit the behavior of all men, Western men included.

Political and economic man, abstractions crucial to the assumptions upon which both realist international relations and liberal political economy have been built, have been constructed out of masculine characteristics—such as autonomy, power, independence, and an instrumental notion of rationality—highly valued in the world of international politics. Realist and economic nationalist explanations of the political and economic behavior of states, as well as prescriptions for their success in the international system, are presented in similar terms. State of nature myths, at the heart of realist assumptions about the international system, which emphasize the dangers of and need to control wild and dangerous spaces, parallel Enlightenment science's attitude toward nature. This view of nature has been an important aspect of the ideological underpinnings of an expansionary Eurocentric state system and a capitalist world economy, as well as of Western projects of political and economic development.

The individual, the state, and the international system, the levels of analysis favored by realists for explaining international conflict, are not merely discrete levels of analysis around which artificial boundaries can be drawn; they are mutually reinforcing constructs, each based on behaviors associated with hegemonic masculinity. While various approaches to international relations critical of realist thinking have questioned the adequacy of these assumptions and explanations of contemporary realities, they have not done so on the basis of gender. Marxist analyses of the world economy are also constructed out of the historical experiences of men in the public world of production. Revealing the masculinist underpinnings of both these types of discourse suggests that realism, as well as the approaches of many of its critics, has constructed worldviews based on the behavior of only half of humanity.

Bringing to light this association between an idealized manhood and international relations reveals the possibility of constructing alternative perspectives divorced from historical associations with masculinity. However, if the worlds of international statecraft and strategic and foreign policy-making are worlds whose key protagonists are mostly men, one could claim that the discipline that describes them is a representation of reality at least with respect to its gender biases. The privileging of concepts such as power and autonomy and the emphasis on war and conflict do conform to patterns of behavior of many states in the international system. However, the feminist perspectives on national security, international political economy, and ecology that I have presented, which are based on different assumptions, demonstrate that there are equally plausible alternative ways of conceptualizing security and prescribing for its realization. They also draw our attention to examining the world from perspectives not of elite decision-makers but of those who are outside positions of power yet can present an equally plausible representation of reality.

While the traditional national security approach is based on the assumption that security demands autonomy and separation, in the highly interdependent world facing the multidimensional threats that I have described, autonomy may no longer be possible or desirable. Feminist approaches offer us new tools with which to question this exclusionary way of thinking. Drawing on experiences more typical of women, feminist theories start with the assumption that striving for attachment and community is as much a part of human nature as is the desire for independence. Conventional international relations thinking, which has prioritized "high politics," or issues relating to international conflict, draws our attention away from other activities in the international system, activities that are closer to behaviors traditionally associated with the feminine. Although it has been devalued in the way in which we usually think about international relations, building community is also an aspect of the political and economic behavior of states in the international system. Assuming the need for interdependence as one part of human behavior allows us to see community building not as an aberration but as another dimension of international behavior. Regional integration schemes, such as the European Community, suggest that we may be moving toward modes of international organization that demand different models of analysis, models not based on an exclusionary definition of national sovereignty.

Realist models of international relations have been built on assumptions of rigid boundary distinctions between outside and inside, anarchy and order, and foreign and domestic. The outside is portrayed in terms of dangerous spaces where violence is unsanctioned. This threat of violence must be guarded against and controlled if security on the inside is to be achieved. Feminist perspectives point to the inadequacy of these boundary distinctions for understanding the roots of conflict and suggest other possible ways of thinking about national security. By emphasizing the interrelationship of violence at all levels of society—as well as its relation to family violence, which also takes place in spaces that are usually beyond the sanction of the law—these feminist perspectives can help us to rethink such boundary distinctions.

Threats of nuclear annihilation and environmental degradation and the interdependence of states in their economic relations all suggest that statist approaches to national security are becoming dysfunctional. We can no longer afford to think in terms of the hierarchical boundary distinctions fostered by the exclusionary we/they attitude of the modern state system. Technologies of modern warfare have broken down boundaries between protectors and protected. Interventionist practices of great powers in the conflicts of weaker states, as well as ethnic strife caused by the lack of coincidence between state boundaries and the various nationalities living within these internationally sanctioned borders, blur distinctions between domestic and international violence. If this feminist analysis has suggested that true security can be achieved only with the elimination of rigid hierarchical gender distinctions, the same conclusion could apply to the hierarchical distinctions through which we have been socialized into thinking about the international system.

Models of economic development and prescriptions for maximizing world welfare have not taken into account women's particular needs or the roles that women play in the world economy. Since women have not been at the center of political and economic decision making, approaches that draw on women's experiences can give us perspectives on security based on standpoints of those outside traditional structures of power. For example, feminist critiques of Marxism emphasize the need to recognize the contribution that women make to production and reproduction in their household roles and in the subsistence economy. They also point to the fact that the exploitation of women's unpaid or underpaid labor has been crucial for the expansion of the capitalist world economy.

Since women are disproportionately located on the peripheries of the international system and at the bottom of the economic scale, feminist perspectives on security prioritize issues associated with the achievement of justice, issues that are frequently ignored in conventional theories of international politics, which have been preoccupied with questions relating to order. While one of the most important goals of feminism is to overcome women's marginalization from institutions of power, women's prominent role in social movements and in new forms of economic production provides examples of new ways of thinking about democratic decentralization, a restructuring of society that offers important alternative models for the achievement of a more comprehensive form of security.

Because women have been peripheral to the institutions of the state and transnational capital, feminist perspectives on international relations must take a critical stance with respect to these institutions, questioning whether they are able to cope with global security problems such as militarism, poverty, and the natural environment. Building a model of political economy that starts at the bottom and takes into account individuals and the local satisfaction of their basic needs envisages a state that is more self-reliant with respect to the international system and more able to live within its own resource limits; such a state would be less militaristic and could therefore give priority to social issues rather than military considerations.[2] Such a model would depend on an extended definition of security that goes beyond a nationalist, militarist focus and begins to speak to the economic and ecological security needs of individuals and states alike.

Concern for the natural environment is an issue that has made a relatively new appearance on the agenda of international politics; yet the rate at which new threats to ecological security are appearing suggests that it is an issue that will demand increasing attention from scholars of international relations in the future. As efforts to manage problems of environmental degradation fail to keep pace with newly discovered threats, ecologists point to more fundamental problems of humans' exploitative attitude toward nature. Ecofeminists have taken an important additional step by making explicit the interrelationship between the historical foundations of modern science's exploitative attitude toward nature, the birth of the modern state and the capitalist world economy, and the separation of gender roles that resulted in the delegitimation of the feminine in public life. Beginning in seventeenth-century Europe, the dichotomization of gender roles has served as an important part of the foundation upon which modern theories of international politics and economics, as well as modern attitudes toward nature, have been constructed. Linking these changing worldviews to the international behavior of modern states and the expansion of the global economy offers us important new ways to think about the interrelationship of political, economic, and ecological insecurities. It also allows us to explain the international behavior of states, not as realists have portrayed it in terms of timeless practices that can be expected to repeat themselves indefinitely into the future, but as behavior constructed out of the value system of the modern West. This historical construction allows us to envisage possibilities for transcending the present system in ways that could offer more secure futures.

Is a Better Future Female?

If characteristics associated with hegemonic masculinity are not serving to increase security in our contemporary world, do more secure futures depend on the substitution of values or characteristics more typically associated with femininity? Certain contemporary feminists have celebrated gender difference and hypothesized a special female world superior to and separate from the world of men. In her book entitled *Is The Future Female?*, Lynne Segal claims that this type of thinking is dangerous and divisive and unlikely to achieve the major goal of feminism, which should be to work for the equality of women.[3] Segal argues that women, whose many gendered identities are constructed in terms of race, class, culture, and historical circumstances, cannot be characterized in these essentialist categories. Contemporary characterizations of women in terms similar to the Victorian ideal of the "good woman" serve only to make men more powerful. The celebration of female virtues supports the view of males as protectors and reinforces the separation between public and private spheres, relegating women to the latter. It also diverts attention from the agenda of working toward women's political, economic, and social equality, an agenda necessary for the achievement of genuine security.

Characteristics that have typically been associated with femininity must therefore be seen not in essentialist terms but as characteristics that women have developed in response to their socialization and their historical roles in society. The association of women with moral virtues such as caring comes not from women's innate moral superiority but from women's activities in the private sphere where these values are accepted in theory, if not always in practice. Since they are linked to women and the private sphere, however, these feminine characteristics have been devalued in the public realm, particularly in the world of international politics. The question then becomes how to revalue them in public life in ways that can contribute to the creation of a more just and secure world. Taking care not to elevate these feminine characteristics to a position of superiority, we can regard them as an inspiration that can contribute to our thinking about ways to build better futures. Even if the better future is not female, a human future that rejects the rigid separation of public and private sphere values and the social distinctions between women and men requires that the good qualities of both are equally honored and made available to all.

In the modern West, women's activities have typically been associated with a devalued world of reproduction and maintenance, while men's have been tied to what have been considered the more elevated tasks of creating history and meaning. Yet all these activities are equally important for human well-being. History and the construction of meaning help us to achieve the kind of security that comes from an understanding of who we are as individuals and as citizens, while reproduction and maintenance are necessary for our survival.

In the discourse of international politics, however, our national identities as citizens have been tied to the heroic deeds of warrior-patriots and our various states' successful participation in international wars. This militarized version of national identity has also depended on a devaluation of the identities of those outside the boundaries of the state.

Additionally, it has all but eliminated the experiences of women from our collective national memories. A less militarized version of national identity, which would serve us better in the contemporary world where advances in technology are making wars as dangerous for winners as for losers, must be constructed out of the equally valued experiences of both women and men. To foster a more peaceful world, this identity must also rest on a better understanding and appreciation of the histories of other cultures and societies.

The multidimensional nature of contemporary insecurities also highlights the importance of placing greater public value on reproduction and maintenance. In a world where nuclear war could destroy the earth and most of its inhabitants, we can no longer afford to celebrate the potential death of hundreds of thousands of our enemies; the preservation of life, not its destruction, must be valued. The elimination of structural violence demands a restructuring of the global economy so that individuals' basic material needs take priority over the desire for profit. An endangered natural environment points to the need to think in terms of the reproduction rather than the exploitation of nature. This ethic of caring for the planet and its inhabitants has been devalued by linking it to the private realm associated with the activities of women; yet caring and responsibility are necessary aspects of all dimensions of life, public and private. They will be valued in the public realm only when men participate equally in the private realm in tasks associated with maintenance and responsibility for child rearing. If we are to move toward a more secure future, what we value in the public realm, including the realm of international politics, should not be so rigidly separated from the values we espouse in the home.

Rewards for men and women for behaviors associated with caring for life in both the public and private spheres should be an important aspect of any redefinition of the meaning of patriotism. Replacing warrior-patriots with citizen-defenders provides us with models that are more conducive to women's equal participation in international poli-

tics. Such a reorientation of patriotism involves what Jean
Elshtain calls undermining the strategic voice, the language
of national security experts. Elshtain claims that this discourse is the preserve of trained experts and is not available
to most citizens, male or female, for the ordinary tasks of
everyday life.[4] Yet it is a language that we are taught to
respect in matters of international politics and one that has
widespread support; to question its authority is considered
unpatriotic.

Looking toward possible alternative futures, R. W. Connell believes that the hegemony of authoritative masculinity
is being disrupted in Western societies. He claims that this
disruption allows us to envisage alternative models of human behavior that are not constructed out of characteristics
that depend on gender inequality.[5] Since the behavior of
states is partly constituted out of the behaviors of their citizens, we might also begin to consider alternative models of
state behavior not constructed out of characteristics associated with hegemonic masculinity. Such models could provide us with a less militarized version of national identity as
well as with a greater appreciation of the identity of others
outside our own state.

In international politics, one model of human behavior
that denies gender inequality could be built around the idea
of mediator rather than warrior. Hypothesizing new models
of masculinity, Mark Gerzon portrays "the Mediator," whom
he describes as one no longer enamored with violence. Gerzon constructs the mediator out of an interview with William
Ury of the Harvard Negotiation Project. Mediators need pa-
tience, empathy, and sensitivity, qualities that Ury recognized as those usually described as feminine.[6] Another such
model is used by social psychologist Herbert Kelman in his
problem-solving workshops that bring together parties in
conflict for purposes of mediation. The goal of these workshops is for each side to try to understand, and see as legitimate, the other's perspective—in other words, to attempt to
break down barriers that rigidly separate parties in interna-

tional conflicts. An important part of this process is building trust. Striving to understand the other's point of view and building trust are not processes that have been valued in the traditional practices of statecraft; they are, however, processes that depend on breaking down political and social hierarchies, including gender hierarchies.[7]

While states' behavior in the international system can often be described in terms similar to characteristics associated with hegemonic masculinity, states do vary across time and space, with respect both to their attitude toward security enhancement and to their attitude toward women, yet rarely have these attitudes been examined together. In an unusual cross-cultural study, which examines the role of values in the choices that states make in selecting development paths, Geert Hofstede uses gender as one of his categories of analysis. In all the societies examined in the study, women were perceived as caring for people and the quality of life. In societies that Hofstede labeled masculine, men tended to see their roles as maximally different from those of women. In societies labeled as feminine, considerable overlap in gender roles was evident; men were less assertive and more oriented toward caring. Hofstede's findings suggest that Scandinavian countries scored high on characteristics he labeled as feminine. In policy terms this has translated into sympathy for the weak at home and support for foreign aid programs abroad. According to Hofstede, both national and international disputes tend to get solved peacefully in such societies.[8]

Although the Scandinavian countries are not widely perceived as significant actors in the international system, their policymakers have often taken leading roles in working for peace and the natural environment, and their foreign aid programs rank among the highest in terms of per capita contributions. These countries also rank high in terms of public policies that serve the interests of women. In an interview with the *New York Times* (May 22, 1991), Gro Brundtland, the prime minister of Norway and the leading author of the Report of the World Commission on Environment and Development, claimed that in Norway, where women hold half the cabinet positions, a much stronger emphasis has been placed on child care, education, and family life than in other states. According to Hofstede, the Scandinavian example suggests that states with less militaristic foreign policies and a greater commitment to economic and ecological security may also rely on less gendered models of national identity.

What Is to Be Done? Beyond a Gendered Perspective on International Relations

In most of the contemporary world men do not need to give up their gender identity in order to practice foreign policy; however, the same cannot be said for women. Until we reach a point where values associated with femininity are more universally valued in public life, women will continue to try to give up being feminine when they enter the world of international politics, for those who are the most successful are those who can best deny their femininity.

Given the generally masculine nature of international politics, how could such a change in values be effected? Underscoring the masculinist orientation in the discipline of international relations does nothing to change the masculinist underpinnings of states' behavior in the international system. In the world of statecraft, no fundamental change in the hierarchy of the sexes is likely to take place until women occupy half, or nearly half, the positions at all levels of foreign and military policy-making. No change in the hierarchy of gender will occur until mediators and care givers are as valued as presidents as citizen-warriors currently are. This will not come about until we have a new vision of international relations and until we live in a world in which gender hierarchies no longer contribute to women's oppression. To the very limited extent they have been visible in the world of international politics, women have generally been perceived as victims or problems; only when women's problems or victimization are seen as being the result of unequal, unjust, or exploitative gender relations can women participate equally with men as agents in the provision of global security.

When women have been politically effective, it has generally been at the local level. Increasingly, women around the world are taking leadership roles in small-scale development projects such as cooperative production and projects designed to save the natural environment. Women are also playing important roles in social movements associated with peace and the environment. While these decentralized democratic projects are vital for women to achieve a sense of empowerment and are important building blocks for a more secure future, they will remain marginal as long as they are seen as women's projects and occur far from centers of power. Hence it is vitally important that women be equally represented, not just in social movements and in local politics but at all levels of policy-making. If foreign policy-making within states has been a difficult area for women to enter, leadership positions in international organizations have been equally inaccessible.

While women must have access to what have traditionally been seen as centers of power where men predominate, it is equally important for women and men to work together at the local level. Victories in local struggles are important for the achievement of the kind of multidimensional, multilevel security I have proposed. The feminist perspectives presented in this book suggest that issues of global security are interconnected with, and partly constituted by, local issues; therefore the achievement of comprehensive security depends on action by women and men at all levels of society. Such action is only possible when rigid gender hierarchies are challenged.

To begin to construct this more secure world requires fundamental changes in the discipline that describes and analyzes world politics. The focus of this book has been on how the discipline of international relations would be changed by the introduction of gender as a category of analysis. To begin to think about how gender might be introduced into the discipline and to recapitulate and extend the arguments made in this book, I shall conclude by drawing on the work of feminist scholar Peggy McIntosh, who outlines five phases of curriculum change necessary for introducing gender into scholarly disciplines. While she uses history as an example, her analysis could equally well apply to the discipline of international relations.[9]

The first phase is what McIntosh describes as a womanless world; this type of analysis describes only the activities of those holding high positions of power, usually in dominant states. It is a mode of analysis that has the effect of reinforcing the existing system. My analysis of traditional approaches to the discipline suggests that this is where most of our conventional teaching about international relations has been situated. Phase two, which also has the effect of reinforcing the existing system, notes the absence of women and adds a famous few to the curriculum. While these additions provide role models for women, they do nothing to change the discipline in ways that acknowledge that anything can be learned from women's experiences; rather, they suggest that women can be recognized by the discipline only if they become like men in the public world.[10] In phase three, the absence of women is seen as a problem as we begin to understand the politics implicit in a curriculum constructed without the inclusion of women's experiences; in this phase, women are typically seen as victims. Moving to phase four involves seeing women as valid human beings whose various life experiences have shaped the world in which we live, even though their contributions involve tasks that are often unacknowledged. The final phase of McIntosh's curriculum development brings us to the point where the subject matter of the discipline genuinely includes the experiences of all individuals regardless of race, culture, class, and gender.

Were it to be realized, such a "re-vision" would have a profound impact on the discipline of international relations, which is noteworthy for its exclusionary perspective both with respect to women as well as to non-Western cultures. As this analysis has suggested, a discipline that includes us all would require a radical redrawing of the boundaries of its subject matter. The absence of women from the study of international relations has been so complete that the masculine orientation of the discipline goes unnoticed by most scholars and students. Yet constructing explanations for their absence is only a first step in realizing a nongendered perspective on international relations. For such a perspective to be achieved, it is necessary to go beyond an investigation of the reasons for women's absence from the subject matter of the discipline by demonstrating the many ways in which women's life experiences have an impact on and are affected by the world of international politics, even if they have been largely invisible. Only through analysis that recognizes gender differences but does not take them as fixed or inevitable can we move toward the creation of a nongendered discipline that includes us all.

Notes

1. Engendered Insecurities

Roosevelt epigraph from speech to the United Nations General Assembly (1952), quoted in Crapol, ed., *Women and American Foreign Policy*, p. 176; de Beauvoir epigraph from *The Second Sex*, p. 161.

1. McGlen and Sarkees, "Leadership Styles of Women in Foreign Policy," p. 17.

2. While Regan's remarks sparked protest at the time, the fact that he could make such comments with relatively little political damage is instructive. Gender stereotyping of the sort that diminishes women remains relatively uncontested in political discourse. Similar comments about minorities or ethnic groups would probably do more damage to politicians' careers.

3. Abzug, "Bella Abzug Enters the House of Representatives," in Barber and Kellerman, eds., *Women Leaders in American Politics*, p. 279.

4. *Boston Globe*, September 29, 1987, p. 1.

5. Crapol, ed., *Women and American Foreign Policy*, p. 167.

6. Connell, *Gender and Power*, ch. 8. Characteris-

NOTES

tics that Connell associates with hegemonic masculinity are also found in some women. The example of former British prime minister Margaret Thatcher would be relevant here; her "macho" qualities during the Falklands/Malvinas war of 1982 reinforced her legitimacy as prime minister and increased her popularity with the British electorate.

7. Scott, *Gender and the Politics of History*, p. 42. Scott's chapter 2, entitled "Gender: A Useful Category of Historical Analysis," on which my analysis of gender draws, was originally published in the *American Historical Review* (December 1986), 91(5):1053–1075.

8. Ibid., p. 43.

9. Broverman et al., "Sex-Role Stereotypes: A Current Appraisal." Although the original study was published in 1972, replication of this research in the 1980s confirmed that these perceptions still held in the United States.

10. Scott, *Gender and the Politics of History*, p. 43

11. As of 1986, a study showed that no major American international relations journal had published any articles that used gender as a category of analysis. See Steuernagel and Quinn, "Is Anyone Listening?" Apart from a special issue of the British international relations journal *Millennium* (Winter 1988), 17(3), on women and international relations, very little attention has been paid to gender in any major international relations journal.

12. Carr, *The Twenty Years' Crisis*, chs. 1 and 2.

13. For a discussion of Kennan's views on this issue, see Hunt, *Ideology and U.S. Foreign Policy*, pp. 5–8.

14. The most cited text in the twentieth-century classical realist tradition is Hans Morgenthau's *Politics Among Nations*. My description of the classical realist tradition draws heavily on this work. Originally published in 1948, *Politics Among Nations* subsequently went through six editions, the last one published in 1985 after Morgenthau's death. Scholars trained in the discipline of international relations who have entered the policy world, such as Henry Kissinger and George Kennan, have generally come out of the classical realist tradition.

15. Holsti, *The Dividing Discipline*, p. 146. Holsti would be hard-pressed to find any "founding mothers" in a field that has been heavily populated by white males.

16. For examples see Small and Singer, *Resort to Arms*, and Deutsch, *Nationalism and Social Communication*.

17. See, for example, Waltz, *Theory of International Politics*.

18. See, for example, Schelling, *The Strategy of Conflict*.

19. Keohane and Nye, *Power and Interdependence*.

20. Wallerstein, *The Modern World-System*, and Cardoso and Faletto, *Dependency and Development in Latin America*.

21. Galtung, "A Structural Theory of Imperialism."

22. Falk, "Contending Approaches to World Order," p. 179.

23. Falk et al., *Toward a Just World Order*.

24. In *Sexism and the War System*, ch. 4, Betty Reardon points out that world order studies scholars and peace researchers are almost all men. She argues that, although little attention has been devoted to gender on the part of these scholars, all the systems of oppression with which world order scholars, peace researchers, and feminists are concerned are structurally interrelated. For a critique of Reardon's position see Sylvester, "Some Dangers in Merging Feminist and Peace Projects."

25. Tong, *Feminist Thought*, p. 2. My description of the varieties of contemporary feminist thought draws heavily on her chapter 1.

26. Ruddick, *Maternal Thinking*, p. 129. See also Hartsock, *Money, Sex, and Power*, ch. 10.

27. Runyan and Peterson, "The Radical Future of Realism," p. 7.

28. Tong, *Feminist Thought*, p. 7

29. Runyan and Peterson, "The Radical Future of Realism," p. 3.

30. Brown, "Feminism, International Theory, and International Relations of Gender Inequality," p. 469.

31. For a summary of these debates see Lapid, "The Third Debate."

32. For a sampling of these writers see *International Studies Quarterly*, Special Issue on "Speaking the Language of Exile and Dissidence in International Studies."

33. Walker, "Contemporary Militarism and the Discourse of Dissent," in Walker, ed., *Culture, Ideology, and World Order*, p. 314.

34. Wallensteen, "The Origins of Peace Research," ch. 1 in Wallensteen, ed., *Peace Research*. For examples of new thinking on security see Ullman, "Redefining Security"; Buzan, *People, States and Fear*; Independent Commission on Disarmament and Security Issues, *Common Security*; Stockholm International Peace Research Institute (SIPRI), *Policies for Common Security*; Azar and Moon, "Third World National Security"; and Mathews, "Redefining Security." This Western new thinking on security parallels some of Mikhail Gorbachev's "new thinking" as outlined in his political report to the Twenty-seventh Party Congress cited in *Pravda*, February 26, 1986.

35. It is interesting to note that women were also among the pioneers in the redefinition of international security. See Boulding, "Women in Peace Studies," in Kramarae and Spender, eds., *The Knowledge Explosion*. Boulding claims that often new ideas do not receive widespread attention in any discipline until they are adopted by men. She also makes the point that the discipline of peace research has been as male dominated as the field of international relations.

36. Brown, "Feminism, International Theory, and International Relations of Gender Inequality," p. 473.

2. Man, the State, and War

De Beauvoir epigraph from *The Second Sex*, p. 72. De Beauvoir's analysis suggests that she herself endorsed this explanation for male superiority; Ruskin epigraph from "Of Queens' Gardens," quoted in Carole Pateman, "Feminist Critiques of the Public/Private Dichotomy," in Benn and Gaus, *Public and Private in Social Life*, p. 291; Fussell epigraph quoted by Anna Quindlen in *The New York Times*, February 7, 1991, p. A25.

1. Waltz, *Theory of International Politics*, p. 102.

2. While heads of state, all men, discussed the "important" issues in world politics at the Group of Seven meeting in London in July 1991, Barbara Bush and Princess Diana were pictured on the "CBS Evening News" (July 17, 1991) meeting with British AIDS patients.

3. By relying on the work of these two authors I do not mean to slight others in the realist tradition. Realism is an old and rich tradition in international relations, the roots of which go back to Thucydides and the classical Greeks. While this chapter will concentrate on the work of two American scholars, the European influence on realism has been considerable. Important realist scholars in the European tradition include Raymond Aron, Martin Wight, Hedley Bull, and Stanley Hoffmann. Morgenthau himself was of European background.

4. Waltz, *Man, the State, and War*, p. 167. Since Waltz's frequently cited discussion of Rousseau's stag hunt was written, some neorealists have tried to reinterpret it in less dire terms, while others have criticized the adequacy of Waltz's rendering of Rousseau. See, for example, Snidal, "Relative Gains and the Pattern of International Cooperation," and Williams, "Rousseau, Realism, and *Realpolitik*."

5. The term *security dilemma* is attributed to John Herz. My analysis of the security dilemma relies on Waltz, *Theory of International Politics*, pp. 186–187.

6. Morgenthau, *Politics Among Nations*, p. 113.

7. Waltz, *Theory of International Politics*, pp. 106–107.

8. Ibid., pp. 170–171.

9. Morgenthau, *Politics Among Nations*, ch. 1.

10. While in *Theory of International Politics* Waltz favors a systems level of analysis, in his earlier work *Man, the State, and War*, he analyzes the way in which all three levels relate to international conflict. For further discussion of levels of analysis see J. David Singer, "The Level-of-Analysis Problem," in Rosenau, ed., *International Politics and Foreign Policy*. More recently, Robert North has conceived of the natural environment as a fourth level of analysis. See North, *War, Peace, Survival*.

11. Waltz, *Theory of International Politics*, ch. 6.

12. Keller, *Reflections on Gender and Science*, p. 130.

13. For example, see Haraway, *Primate Visions*, ch. 1. Considering scientific practice from the perspective of the way its factual findings are narrated, Haraway provocatively explores how scientific theories produce and are embedded in particular kinds of stories. This allows her to chal-

lenge the neutrality and objectivity of scientific facts. She suggests that texts about primates can be read as science fictions about race, gender, and nature.

14. Morgenthau, *Politics Among Nations*, p. 34.

15. Morgenthau does talk about dominating mothers-in-law, but as feminist research has suggested, it is generally men, legally designated as heads of households in most societies, who hold the real power even in the family and certainly with respect to the family's interaction with the public sphere.

16. For an extended discussion of Morgenthau's "political man," see Tickner, "Hans Morgenthau's Principles of Political Realism. " In neorealism's depersonalized structural analysis, Morgenthau's depiction of human nature slips out of sight.

17. Brown, *Manhood and Politics*, pp. 43–59.

18. Jean Elshtain suggests that in Athens and Sparta this notion of heroic sacrifice was extended to women who died in childbirth producing citizens for the state. See Elshtain, "Sovereignty, Identity, Sacrifice," in Peterson, ed., *Gendered States*.

19. Brown, *Manhood and Politics*, ch. 5.

20. Pitkin, *Fortune Is a Woman*, p. 22.

21. Brown, *Manhood and Politics*, p. 82.

22. Pitkin, *Fortune Is a Woman*, ch. 6.

23. Brown, *Manhood and Politics*, pp. 80–88.

24. Machiavelli, *The Prince and the Discourses*, p. 94.

25. For example, he states in the *Art of War*, book 6, that women must not be allowed into a military camp, for they "make soldiers rebellious and useless." Quoted in Pitkin, *Fortune Is a Woman*, p. 72.

26. Kathleen Jones, "Dividing the Ranks: Women and the Draft," ch. 6 in Elshtain and Tobias, eds., *Women, Militarism, and War*, p. 126.

27. Gerzon, *A Choice of Heroes*, p. 31.

28. A *New York Times* interview, January 22, 1991, p. A12, with Sgt. Cheryl Stewart serving in the Gulf, revealed that she was close to divorce because her husband's ego had been bruised by remaining home with the couple's children.

29. Elshtain, *Women and War*, p. 207. Elshtain is citing a study by the military historian S. L. A. Marshall. This figure is, however, disputed by other analysts.

30. Stiehm, "The Protected, the Protector, the Defender," in Stiehm, *Women and Men's Wars*, p. 371.

31. Tobias, "Shifting Heroisms: The Uses of Military Service in Politics," ch. 8 in Elshtain and Tobias, eds., *Women, Militarism, and War*. Tobias uses Daniel Quayle as an example of a politician who, in the 1988 U.S. election, suffered from the perception that he had avoided military service.

32. *New York Times*, February, 11, 1991, p. A12. In an interview with

American troops assembling bombs in the Saudi desert during the 1991 Persian Gulf war, Dan Rather on the "CBS Evening News," (February 19, 1991) described how each bomb bore a personal message to Saddam Hussein. It has been customary in military discourse to refer to the missiles themselves as "he." Nuclear weapons have even been given boys' or men's names: the bombs dropped over Nagasaki and Hiroshima were nicknamed Fat Man and Little Boy.

33. In a military briefing on the last day of the Persian Gulf war, General Norman Schwarzkopf, when describing the allied ground campaign, referred to a "Hail Mary" move in football. "McNeil/Lehrer Report," February 27, 1991.

34. *Games Nations Play* is the title of a popular textbook in international relations by John Spanier. To describe the "game" of international relations, Raymond Aron used the metaphor of a soccer game without defined boundaries, mutually agreed-upon rules, or an impartial referee to enforce them. See Aron, *Peace and War*, pp. 8–10.

35. Morgenthau, *Politics Among Nations*, p. 353.

36. Ashley, "The Poverty of Neorealism," ch. 9 in Keohane, ed., *Neorealism and Its Critics*, p. 258.

37. Elshtain, *Women and War*, p. 91.

38. Tilly, "Reflections on the History of European State-Making" ch. 1 in Tilly, ed., *The Formation of National States in Western Europe*.

39. Soon after the outbreak of the Persian Gulf war in 1991, the *Boston Globe* (January 22, 1991, p. 1) reported that the war had dramatically boosted Americans' self-image: before the war 32 percent of Americans felt good about the country; after two days of fighting the figure nearly doubled to 62 percent. Figures are from a Gallup poll.

40. Speaking of the Persian Gulf war, Gordon Adams of the Defense Budget Project said: "It's not cheap, but it is a pretty small price tag to pay for a pretty large effort. . . . Other people will tell you, 'I wanted to spend that on child care' but that is not what is going on here." *Boston Globe*, January 19, 1991, p. 1.

41. The study also revealed a high rate of sexual harassment of women, a condition that is widespread in the military services.

42. Stiehm, *Arms and the Enlisted Woman*, p. 174.

43. For example, Cynthia Enloe asserts that military nurses suffer from invisibility; the army does not want them to talk because they see the horror of war in the wounded. Enloe, *Does Khaki Become You?*, ch. 4. The 1991 Gulf war intensified the debate in the United States about the suitability of women for combat. In May 1991 the U.S. House of Representatives passed a bill, sponsored by Representative Patricia Schroeder, that allows (but does not require) women Air Force pilots to fly in combat. *Boston Globe*, May 23, 1991, p. 1.

44. *Newsweek*, July 1, 1991.

45. Cohn, "Sex and Death in the Rational World of Defense Intellectuals."

46. Cohn, "Emasculating America's Linguistic Deterrent," ch. 8 in Harris and King, eds., *Rocking the Ship of State*, p. 154.

47. Ashley, "Untying the Sovereign State," p. 230.

48. Hobbes, *Leviathan*, part 1, ch. 13, quoted in Vasquez, ed., *Classics of International Relations*, pp. 213–215.

49. Pateman, *The Sexual Contract*, p. 41.

50. Flax, "Political Philosophy and the Patriarchal Unconscious: A Psychoanalytic Perspective on Epistemology and Metaphysics," in Harding and Hintikka, eds., *Discovering Reality*, pp. 245–281.

51. Di Stephano, "Masculinity as Ideology in Political Theory." Carole Pateman has disputed some of Di Stephano's assumptions about Hobbes's characterizations of women and the family in the state of nature. But this does not deny the fact that Di Stephano's characterization of men is the one used by realists in their depiction of the international system. See Pateman, " 'God Hath Ordained to Man a Helper': Hobbes, Patriarchy, and Conjugal Right."

52. Critics of realism have questioned whether the Hobbesian analogy fits the international system. See, for example, Beitz, *Political Theory and International Relations*, pp. 35–50.

53. Pitkin, *Fortune Is a Woman*, p. 127.

54. Ruddick, *Maternal Thinking*, p. 152.

55. Higonnet et al., *Behind the Lines*, introduction.

56. Elshtain, *Women and War*, p. 194.

57. Ibid., p. 168.

58. Enloe, *Bananas, Beaches, and Bases*, pp. 48–49.

59. Hunt, *Ideology and U.S. Foreign Policy*, pp. 58–62.

60. Ibid., p. 164.

61. At Hiroshima 90 percent of the victims were civilians. The military's answer to this problem is the production of "smart bombs," which can be aimed precisely at military targets. Given the ever-increasing level of destruction of modern technologies and escalating arms acquisitions, this does not seem like the most stable way to provide security.

62. *Common Security*, introduction by Olof Palme, pp. xi–xvii. The end of the Cold War has not eliminated these dangers. The fear of accidental firing of strategic nuclear weapons belonging to the United States and nuclear states of the former Soviet Union remains. Nuclear proliferation and the spread of other weapons of mass destruction also contribute to the fear of use of these weapons, which, paradoxically, are supposed to increase security.

63. Wilson and Wallensteen, *Major Armed Conflicts in 1987*. This report notes that at the end of 1987 only one of thirty-six major armed conflicts was taking place outside the Third World.

64. Jackson and Rosberg, "Why Africa's Weak States Persist," p. 23.
65. *Common Security: A Blueprint for Survival*, p. xiii.
66. Addams et al., *Women at The Hague*, pp. 150ff.
67. Runyan, "Feminism, Peace, and International Politics," ch. 6.
68. "Forward-looking Strategies for the Advancement of Women Towards the Year 2000." Quoted in Pietilä and Vickers, *Making Women Matter*, pp. 46–47.
69. Boulding, "Women in Peace Studies" in Kramarae and Spender, eds., *The Knowledge Explosion*.
70. Reardon, *Sexism and the War System*, ch. 1.
71. Connell, *Gender and Power*, p. 129, portrays streets as "zones of occupation" by men, there being no such thing as "women's streets."
72. Radford, "Policing Male Violence—Policing Women" ch. 3 in Hanmer and Maynard, eds., *Women, Violence, and Social Control*, p. 33. Radford reports that in a survey conducted in the London borough of Wandsworth in 1983–84, 88 percent of women said their neighborhood was not safe for women during the night, and 25 percent found it unsafe during the day; large numbers said they went out only when absolutely necessary.
73. Mies, *Patriarchy and Accumulation on a World Scale*, p. 147.
74. Brock-Utne, *Feminist Perspectives on Peace and Peace Education*, p. 50.
75. Gee, "Ensuring Police Protection for Battered Women," p. 555.
76. In its definition of peace already discussed, the Forward-looking Strategy document, adopted at Nairobi in 1985, points to this interrelationship between all types of violence. See Pietilä and Vickers, *Making Women Matter*, pp. 46–47.
77. Breines and Gordon, "The New Scholarship on Family Violence," pp. 492–493.
78. Stiehm, *Arms and the Enlisted Woman*, p. 228.
79. See Elshtain, *Women and War*, ch. 3.
80. Carroll, "Feminism and Pacifism: Historical and Theoretical Connections," in Pierson, ed., *Women and Peace*, pp. 2–28.
81. Margaret Hobbs, "The Perils of 'Unbridled Masculinity': Pacifist Elements in the Feminist and Socialist Thought of Charlotte Perkins Gilman," in Pierson, ed., *Women and Peace*, pp. 149–169.
82. Stiehm, *Women and Men's Wars*, p. 367.
83. Nathanson, "In Defense of 'Moderate Patriotism,' " p. 538.
84. Elshtain and Tobias, eds., *Women, Militarism, and War*, p. xi.
85. Segal, *Is the Future Female?*, p. 165.
86. Ruddick, "The Rationality of Care," ch. 11 in Elshtain and Tobias, eds., *Women, Militarism, and War*.
87. The *New York Times* of December 12, 1990 (p. A35) reported that while men were about evenly split on attacking Iraqi forces in Kuwait, women were 73 percent against and 22 percent in favor.

88. Suzanne Gordon, "Another Enemy," *Boston Globe*, March 8, 1991, p. 15.

89. Brown, *Manhood and Politics*, p. 206.

90. Elshtain, "Sovereignty, Identity, Sacrifice," in Peterson, ed., *Gendered States*.

91. I am grateful to Michael Capps, historian at the Lewis and Clark Museum in St. Louis, Missouri, for this information. The story of Sacajawea is told in one of the museum's exhibits.

92. In *Man, the State, and War*, Waltz argues that "in the stag-hunt example, the will of the rabbit-snatcher was rational and predictable from his own point of view" (p. 183), while "in the early state of nature, men were sufficiently dispersed to make any pattern of cooperation unnecessary" (p. 167). Neorealist revisionists, such as Snidal (see note 4 of this chapter), do not question the masculine bias of the stag hunt metaphor. Like Waltz and Rousseau, they also assume the autonomous, adult male (unparented and in an environment without women or children) in their discussion of the stag hunt; they do not question the rationality of the rabbit-snatching defector or the restrictive situational descriptions implied by their payoff matrices. Transformations in the social nature of an interaction are very hard to represent using such a model. Their reformulation of Waltz's position is instead focused on the exploration of different specifications of the game payoff in less conflictual ways (i.e., as an assurance game) and on inferences concerning the likely consequences of relative gain-seeking behavior in a gamelike interaction with more than two (equally autonomous and unsocialized) players.

93. For a feminist interpretation that disputes this assumption see Mona Harrington, "What Exactly Is Wrong with the Liberal State as an Agent of Feminist Change?," in Peterson, ed., *Gendered States*.

94. Enloe, *Bananas, Beaches, and Bases*, ch. 5. Enloe points out that women, although very underrepresented in the U.S. State Department, make up half the professional staff of the Office of the U.S. Trade Representative. Trade negotiations are an arena in which negotiating skills are particularly valuable, and Enloe believes that women are frequently assigned to these positions because the opposing party is more likely to trust them.

95. In her analysis of difference in men's and women's conversational styles, Deborah Tannen describes life from a male perspective as a struggle to preserve independence and avoid failure. In contrast, for women life is a struggle to preserve intimacy and avoid isolation. Tannen claims that all humans need both intimacy and independence but that women tend to focus on the former and men on the latter. Tannen, *You Just Don't Understand*, pp. 25–26.

96. Keller, *Reflections on Gender and Science*, ch. 3.

97. Reardon, *Sexism and the War System*, p. 88.

98. Keller, *Gender and Science*, p. 117.

99. Harding, *The Science Question in Feminism*, ch. 7.

100. Arendt, *On Violence*, p. 44.

101. McClelland, "Power and the Feminine Role," in McClelland, *Power: The Inner Experience*, ch. 3.

102. Jaquette, "Power as Ideology: A Feminist Analysis," in Stiehm, *Women's Views of the Political World of Men*, ch. 2.

3. Models of Man

Galbraith epigraph quoted in Waring, *If Women Counted*, p. 277; Jain epigraph quoted in Pietilä and Vickers, *Making Women Matter*, p. 35; Perez de Cuellar, secretary general of the United Nations, quoted in the *New York Times*, June 16, 1991, p. A7.

1. Gilpin, *The Political Economy of International Relations*, ch. 2. Gilpin uses the term *nationalism* rather than *economic nationalism*. I shall use *economic nationalism* to distinguish this approach from the international relations literature on nation building.

2. Marianne A. Ferber and Michelle L. Teiman, "The Oldest, the Most Established, the Most Quantitative of the Social Sciences—and the Most Dominated by Men: The Impact of Feminism on Economics," ch. 9 in Spender, ed., *Men's Studies Modified*. The authors note that in the U.S. in 1980 only 8 percent of Ph.D.'s in economics were awarded to women and that women made up only 5 percent of full-time economics faculties in institutions of higher learning.

3. Just as I used the term *political man* in chapter 2, I shall use the term *economic man* or *rational economic man* in this chapter. Since liberal economics has constructed *rational economic man* out of activities historically associated with men in the public sphere of production, I shall retain this gendered construction to emphasize this masculine identification.

4. Hartsock, *Money, Sex, and Power*, p. 47.

5. Harding, *The Science Question in Feminism*, pp. 167–179.

6. Hartsock, *Money, Sex, and Power*, p. 41.

7. Harding, *The Science Question in Feminism*, p. 171.

8. Jaggar, *Feminist Politics and Human Nature*, pp. 40–48.

9. Gill and Law, *The Global Political Economy*, p. 364.

10. Jaggar, *Feminist Politics and Human Nature*, p. 138.

11. Connell, *Gender and Power*, p. 7. Some results from the study quoted in Connell were as follows: for West Germany, women's wages as a percentage of men's were 73 percent; for Japan, 43 percent; for Egypt, 63 percent; for El Salvador, 81 percent; and for Poland, 67 percent. In the United States in 1987 women who worked full time made 71 percent of what men earned (Okin, *Justice, Gender, and the Family*, p. 144).

12. For a review of this literature see Jaquette, "Women and Moderni-

zation Theory." The marginalization of this literature from mainstream development theory tends to reinforce women's isolation and their characterization as victims rather than agents.

13. Boserup, *Women's Role in Economic Development*, ch. 3.

14. Sen and Grown, *Development, Crises, and Alternative Visions*, p. 34. The DAWN group, founded by Devaki Jain, comprises twenty-two Third World women researchers and activists who decided to prepare an independent report of world development for the Nairobi Conference from a Third World women's perspective. This report is the result.

15. Dankelman and Davidson, *Women and Environment in the Third World*, ch. 2.

16. A 1991 Report of the U.N. International Fund for Agricultural Development (IFAD) reported that the number of rural women living in poverty in Third World countries increased 50 percent over the last two decades and that women far outnumber men in such straits. This increase has occurred despite economic gains made by many of these countries. The report claims that, while women form the backbone of agricultural labor in many areas, their contributions remain invisible. Reported in the *Boston Globe*, July 29, 1991, p. 2.

17. Pasuk Phongpaichit, "Two Roads to the Factory: Industrialization Strategies and Women's Employment in South-East Asia," in Agarwal, ed., *Structures of Patriarchy*, pps. 151–163.

18. Enloe, *Bananas, Beaches, and Bases*, ch. 7.

19. For a detailed analysis of the effects of the International Monetary Fund's policies of structural adjustment on women see Vickers, *Women and the World Economic Crisis*, ch. 2.

20. See, for example, Gilpin, *The Political Economy of International Relations*, and Stephen Krasner, "American Policy and Global Economic Stability," ch. 2 in Avery and Rapkin, eds., *America in a Changing World Political Economy*.

21. Gill and Law, *The Global Political Economy*, p. 367.

22. Mitchell, "Women and Equality," ch. 1 in Phillips, ed., *Feminism and Equality*, p. 31.

23. Connell, *Gender and Power*, p. 153.

24. Mies, *Patriarchy and Accumulation on a World Scale*, p. 83.

25. Leonore Davidoff, "Adam Spoke First and Named the Orders of the World: Masculine and Feminine Domains in History and Sociology," in Corr and Jamieson, eds., *The Politics of Everyday Life*, p. 234.

26. Keller, *Reflections on Gender and Science*, chs. 3 and 4.

27. See for example Axelrod, *The Evolution of Cooperation*, and Keohane, *After Hegemony*, pp. 67–84. A Prisoner's Dilemma game is derived from a story about two imprisoned suspects allowed to negotiate their pleas only with a powerful district attorney. Particular configurations of utility payoffs derive from this story. Specifically, it is assumed that for each player T

(temptation payoff associated with his or her defection and the other's cooperation) > R (the reward individually received for joint cooperation) > P (the individual penalty of both players' defection) > S (the "sucker" payoff associated with his or her cooperation and the other's defection). Sometimes the simplifying constraint that $2R > S+T$ is also assumed.

28. Brock-Utne, "Gender and Cooperation in the Laboratory." Brock-Utne cites other recent research that suggests that women may be more influenced by the interpersonal situation, such as getting along with other players, than by strategy considerations associated with winning the game. This is consistent with Deborah Tannen's claim that women in conversation prioritize relationships. See Tannen, *You Just Don't Understand*.

29. Seager and Olson, *Women in the World*, p. 28.

30. Pierce, "The Feminization of Poverty," p. 1.

31. Gill and Law, *The Global Political Economy*, pp. 54–69.

32. This is one of the central claims of Galtung's analysis in "A Structural Theory of Imperialism."

33. Jaggar, *Feminist Politics and Human Nature*, pp. 63–69.

34. Ibid., p. 75.

35. For an extended analysis of this issue, see Waring, *If Women Counted*.

36. Okin, *Justice, Gender, and the Family*, p. 153.

37. Mies, *Patriarchy and Accumulation on a World Scale*, pp. 100–110.

38. Ibid., p. 115.

39. Ibid., p. 31.

40. Sen, "More Than 100 Million Women Are Missing," p. 66.

41. Molyneux, "Mobilization Without Emancipation?"

42. Moore, *Feminism and Anthropology*, pp. 141–142.

43. Hansson and Liden, *Moscow Women*. These interviews suggest that these women preferred the traditional role of housewife to the double burden of working outside the home as well as taking care of a family.

44. Kaldor, "The Global Political Economy," p. 454.

45. Mies, *Patriarchy and Accumulation on a World Scale*, ch. 2.

46. Waring, *If Women Counted*, ch. 11.

47. Okin, *Gender and Justice*, pp. 171ff.

48. For an extended analysis of such a self-reliant development strategy see Tickner, *Self-Reliance Versus Power Politics*.

49. Goetz, "Feminism and the Limits of the Claim to Know," pp. 482–483.

50. Mies, *Patriarchy and Accumulation on a World Scale*, pp. 211ff.

4. Man over Nature

Dalai Lama epigraph quoted in the *Boston Globe*, September 17, 1990, p. 27; Richard Darman, director of Office of Management and Budget, epigraph quoted in the *New York Times*, May 14, 1990, p. A16.

NOTES

1. Quoted in Sprout and Sprout, *The Context of Environmental Politics,* p. 58.

2. Orr and Soroos, eds., *The Global Predicament,* p. 4.

3. For an overview of how various approaches to feminist theory deal with the natural environment see Carolyn Merchant, "Ecofeminism and Feminist History," in Diamond and Orenstein, eds., *Reweaving the World,* pp. 100–105.

4. Morgenthau, *Politics Among Nations.* Originally published in 1948, well before the environment was on the international agenda, *Politics Among Nations* has gone through six editions, all of which have adopted essentially the same attitude toward the natural environment.

5. For an ecological analysis of international conflict and war, an unusual perspective in international relations theory, see Choucri and North, *Nations in Conflict.*

6. White, "The Historical Roots of Our Ecological Crisis."

7. Merchant, *The Death of Nature,* p. 2.

8. Ibid., p. 216.

9. Ritvo, *The Animal Estate,* p. 1.

10. Ibid., p. 11–13.

11. See for example, ibid., p. 3, where Ritvo discusses dog breeders' assumptions about the sexual behavior of dogs, which are loaded with assumptions about human females.

12. Francis Bacon, "The Masculine Birth of Time," quoted in Keller, *Reflections on Gender and Science,* p. 36.

13. Leiss, *The Domination of Nature,* ch. 1.

14. Harding, *The Science Question in Feminism,* p. 113.

15. Keller, *Reflections on Gender and Science,* pp. 63–64.

16. Merchant, *The Death of Nature,* p. 168.

17. Keller, *Reflections on Gender and Science,* p. 61.

18. Merchant, *The Death of Nature,* pp. 65–66.

19. Jack D. Salmon, "Resupplying Spaceship Earth: Prospects for Space Industrialization," ch. 11 in Orr and Soroos, eds., *The Global Predicament.*

20. Leiss, *The Domination of Nature,* ch. 4.

21. Charles Darwin quoted in Ritvo, *The Animal Estate,* p. 16.

22. Ibid., p. 25. African killer bees are a contemporary version of this argument.

23. Merchant, *The Death of Nature,* p. 288.

24. Shiva, *Staying Alive,* p. 85.

25. Merchant, *Ecological Revolutions.*

26. Shiva, *Staying Alive,* p. 19.

27. Merchant, *Ecological Revolutions,* ch. 2

28. Ibid., ch. 7.

29. Ibid., p. 50.

30. Dalby, "American Security Discourse," p. 172.

31. Parker, *Western Geopolitical Thought in the Twentieth Century*, p. 2.
32. Ibid., p. 11.
33. Merchant, *The Death of Nature*, pp. 209–215.
34. Ibid., chs. 8 and 9.
35. The World Commission on Environment and Development, *Our Common Future*, p. 1.
36. Mische, "Ecological Security and the Need to Reconceptualize Sovereignty," p. 389.
37. Sprout and Sprout, *Toward a Politics of the Planet Earth*, ch. 11.
38. Ibid., p. 424.
39. Renner, "National Security," p. 37.
40. Meadows et al., *The Limits to Growth*.
41. For a feminist critique of this single-earth image, see Yaakov Jerome Garb, "Perspective or Escape? Ecofeminist Musings on Contemporary Earth Imagery," in Diamond and Orenstein, eds., *Reweaving the World*, pp. 264–278. Garb claims that this extraterrestrial view of the world, since it relies exclusively on visual imagery that distances subject from object, is a patriarchal form of knowledge that objectifies the earth in the same way that women have been objectified.
42. For an extended critique from this perspective see Hayward R. Alker, Jr., and Ann Tickner, "Some Issues Raised by Previous Models," ch. 4 in Deutsch et al., *Problems of World Modeling*.
43. The World Commission on Environment and Development, *Our Common Future*, ch. 2.
44. Renner, "National Security," p. 30.
45. The World Commission on Environment and Development, *Our Common Future*, p. 292.
46. Mathews, "Redefining Security," p. 166.
47. Hare, "Black Ecology," ch. 12 in Pursell, ed., *From Conservation to Ecology*.
48. Pietilä and Vickers, *Making Women Matter*, p. 129.
49. Dankelman and Davidson, *Women and the Environment in the Third World*, p. 69.
50. Lin Nelson, "The Place of Women in Polluted Places," in Diamond and Orenstein, eds., *Reweaving the World*, p. 180.
51. Pirages, *Global Technopolitics*, ch. 1.
52. Sprout and Sprout, *Toward a Politics of the Planet Earth*, ch. 1.
53. Ibid., p. 128.
54. Botkin, *Discordant Harmonies*.
55. Botkin's description of the science of ecology parallels Evelyn Fox Keller's description of the scientific methodology of biologist Barbara McClintock, which, Keller claims, is different from the methodology of much of modern science. See Keller, *A Feeling for the Organism*.

56. David W. Orr, "Modernization and the Ecological Perspective," ch. 4 in Orr and Soroos, eds., *The Global Predicament*.

57. Dankelman and Davidson, *Women and Environment in the Third World*, ch. 2. See also Shiva, *Staying Alive*, ch. 5.

58. Mische, "Ecological Security and the Need to Reconceptualize Sovereignty," p. 404.

59. Orr, "Modernization and the Ecological Perspective," ch. 4 in Orr and Soroos, eds., *The Global Predicament*, p. 85.

60. Sprout and Sprout, *The Context of Environmental Politics*, ch. 3.

61. Leiss, *The Domination of Nature*, p. 22.

62. Ibid., pp. 120–122.

63. Bookchin, *Toward an Ecological Society*. See also Bookchin, *The Ecology of Freedom*.

64. Socialist feminists, particularly, have criticized what they see as an idealist, antirationalist connection between women and nature. As an example of one such text, see Griffin, *Woman and Nature*.

65. Carol P. MacCormack, "Nature, Culture, and Gender: A Critique," ch. 1 in MacCormack and Strathern, eds., *Nature, Culture, and Gender*. In arguing for a social constructionist position, these authors are critiquing an important piece by Sherry B. Ortner, "Is Female to Male as Nature Is to Culture?," in Rosaldo and Lamphere, eds., *Woman, Culture, and Society*, pp. 67–87. Ortner acknowledges the influence of de Beauvoir on her work. However, to be fair to de Beauvoir, her famous statement that one is not born a woman but becomes one, confirms her belief in the social construction of gender. See de Beauvoir, *The Second Sex*, p. 301.

66. King, "The Ecology of Feminism and the Feminism of Ecology," ch. 2 in Plant, ed., *Healing the Wounds*.

67. Griscom, "On Healing the Nature/History Split in Feminist Thought," p. 5.

68. King, "Feminism and the Revolt of Nature," p. 14.

69. For other examples see Dankelman and Davidson, *Women and Environment in the Third World* and Shiva, *Staying Alive*.

5. Toward a Nongendered Perspective

Pathah epigraph quoted in Dankelman and Davidson, *Women and Environment in the Third World*, p. 171; Kirkpatrick epigraph quoted in Crapol, *Women and American Foreign Policy*, p. 153; Coffin epigraph quoted in Reardon, *Sexism and the War System*, p. 51.

1. For a postmodern analysis that denies the claim that various forms of oppression are necessarily connected, see Laclau and Mouffe, *Hegemony and Socialist Strategy*.

2. For the development of such a model see Tickner, *Self-Reliance Versus Power Politics*, ch. 8.

3. Segal, *Is the Future Female?*, introduction.

4. Elshtain, *Women and War*, p. 245.

5. Connell, *Gender and Power*, ch. 13.

6. Gerzon, *A Choice of Heroes*, p. 248.

7. Kelman, "Interactive Problem Solving: A Social-Psychological Approach to Conflict Resolution," in Klassen, ed., *Dialogue Toward Inter-Faith Understanding*.

8. Hofstede, "The Role of Cultural Values in Economic Development," in Arvedson, Lönnroth, and Rydén, eds., *Economics and Values*, pp. 122–135. Hofstede claims that both the United States and the former Soviet Union have strongly masculine value systems.

9. McIntosh, "Interactive Phases of Curricular Re-Vision."

10. An example of this attitude can be found in a recent international relations undergraduate textbook that contains a picture of former British prime minister Margaret Thatcher riding in a tank during a NATO exercise. The author notes that since two of Thatcher's most important achievements were the war against Argentina in 1982 and the doubling of the number of British troops facing Iraq in 1990, women cannot be expected to change the way in which we conduct international politics. Rourke, *International Politics on the World Stage*, p. 86.

Bibliography

Addams, Jane, Emily G. Balch, and Alice Hamilton. *Women at The Hague: The International Congress of Women and Its Results.* New York: Macmillan, 1916.

Agarwal, Bina, ed. *Structures of Patriarchy: The State, the Community, and the Household.* London: Zed Books, 1990.

Ardener, Shirley, ed. *Perceiving Women.* New York: Wiley, 1975.

Arendt, Hannah. *On Violence.* New York: Harcourt, Brace and World, 1969.

Aron, Raymond. *Peace and War: A Theory of International Relations.* Garden City, N.Y.: Doubleday, 1966.

Arvedson, Ingemund Hägg, Måns Lönnroth, and Bengt Rydén, eds. *Economics and Values.* Stockholm: Almqvist and Wiksell International, 1986.

Ashley, Richard K. "Untying the Sovereign State: A Double Reading of the Anarchy Problematique." *Millennium: Journal of International Studies* 17(2) (1988): 227–262.

Avery, William and David Rapkin, eds. *America in a Changing World Political Economy.* New York: Longman, 1982.

Axelrod, Robert. *The Evolution of Cooperation.* New York: Basic Books, 1984.

Azar, Edward and Chung-in Moon. "Third World National Security: Toward a New Conceptual Framework." *International Interactions* 11(2) (1984): 103–135.

Bandarage, Asoka. "Women in Development: Liberalism, Marxism, and Marxist-Feminism." *Development and Change* 15 (1984): 495–515.

Barber, James David and Barbara Kellerman, eds. *Women Leaders in American Politics.* Eaglewood Cliffs, N.J: Prentice Hall, 1986.

Beauvoir, Simone de. *The Second Sex.* New York: Knopf, 1952.

Beitz, Charles. *Political Theory and International Relations.* Princeton: Princeton University Press, 1979.

Benn, S. I. and G. F. Gaus. *Public and Private in Social Life.* London: Croom Helm, 1983.

Bookchin, Murray. *The Ecology of Freedom.* Palo Alto, Calif.: Cheshire Books, 1982.

Bookchin, Murray. *Toward an Ecological Society.* Montreal: Black Rose Books, 1980.

Boserup, Esther. *Women's Role in Economic Development.* Aldershot, England: Gower, 1986.

Botkin, Daniel B. *Discordant Harmonies: A New Ecology for the Twenty First Century.* New York: Oxford University Press, 1990.

Boulding, Elise. *Women in the Twentieth Century World.* New York: Wiley, 1977.

Breines, Wini and Linda Gordon. "The New Scholarship on Family Violence." *Signs: Journal of Women in Culture and Society* 8(3) (Spring 1983): 490–531.

Brock-Utne, Birgit. *Educating for Peace: A Feminist Perspective.* New York: Pergamon Press, 1985.

Brock-Utne, Birgit. *Feminist Perspectives on Peace and Peace Education.* New York: Pergamon Press, 1989.

Brock-Utne, Birgit. "Gender and Cooperation in the Laboratory." *Journal of Peace Research* 26(1) (1989): 47–56.

Brown, Sarah. "Feminism, International Theory, and International Relations of Gender Inequality." *Millennium: Journal of International Studies* 17(3) (1988): 461–475.

Brown, Wendy. *Manhood and Politics: A Feminist Reading in Political Theory.* Totowa, N.J.: Rowman and Littlefield, 1988.

Broverman, Inge K., Susan R. Vogel, Donald M. Broverman, Frank E. Clarkson, and Paul S. Rosenkranz. "Sex-Role Stereotypes: A Current Appraisal." *Journal of Social Issues* 28(2) (1972): 59–78.

Buzan, Barry. *People, States, and Fear,* 2d ed. Boulder: Lynne Rienner, 1991.

BIBLIOGRAPHY

Cardoso, Fernando and Enzo Faletto. *Dependency and Development in Latin America*. Berkeley: University of California Press, 1979.

Carr, E. H. *The Twenty Years' Crisis, 1919–1939: An Introduction to the Study of International Relations*. New York: Harper & Row, 1964.

Carson, Rachel. *Silent Spring*. London: Hamish Hamilton, 1964.

Charlton, Sue Ellen M. *Women in Third World Development*. Boulder: Westview, 1984.

Choucri, Nazli and Robert C. North. *Nations in Conflict: National Growth and International Violence*. San Francisco: W. H. Freeman, 1975.

Cohn, Carol. "Sex and Death in the Rational World of Defense Intellectuals." *Signs: Journal of Women in Culture and Society* 12(4) (1987): 687–718.

Common Security: A Blueprint for Survival. New York: Simon and Schuster, 1982.

Connell, R. W. *Gender and Power: Society, the Person and Sexual Politics*. Stanford: Stanford University Press, 1987.

Corr, Helen and Lynn Jamieson, eds. *Politics of Everyday Life: Continuity and Change in Work and the Family*. New York: St. Martin's Press, 1990.

Crapol, Edward P., ed. *Women and American Foreign Policy: Lobbyists, Critics, and Insiders*. New York: Greenwood Press, 1987.

Dalby, Simon. "American Security Discourse: The Persistence of Geopolitics." *Political Geography Quarterly* 9(2) (April 1990): 171–188.

Dankelman, Irene and Joan Davidson. *Women and Environment in the Third World: Alliance for the Future*. London: Earthscan Publications, 1988.

Deutsch, Karl W. *Nationalism and Social Communication*. Cambridge, Mass.: M.I.T. Press, 1954.

Deutsch, Karl W., Bruno Fritsch, Helio Jaguaribe, and Andrei S. Markovits, eds. *Problems of World Modeling: Political and Social Implications*. Cambridge, Mass.: Ballinger, 1977.

Diamond, Irene and Gloria Feman Orenstein, eds. *Reweaving the World: The Emergence of Ecofeminism*. San Francisco: Sierra Club Books, 1990.

Dietz, Mary G. "Context Is All: Feminism and Theories of Citizenship." *Daedelus* 116(4) (Fall 1987): 1–24.

Di Stephano, Christine. "Masculinity as Ideology in Political Theory: Hobbesian Man Considered." *Women's Studies International Forum* 6(6) (1983): 633–644.

Eisler, Riane. *The Chalice and the Blade: Our History, Our Future*. San Francisco: Harper & Row, 1988.

Elshtain, Jean Bethke. *Public Man, Private Woman: Women in Social and Political Thought*. Oxford: Martin Robertson, 1981.

Elshtain, Jean Bethke. "Reflections on War and Political Discourse: Realism, Just War, and Feminism in the Nuclear Age." *Political Theory* 13(1) (February 1985): 39–57.

Elshtain, Jean Bethke. *Women and War*. New York: Basic Books, 1987.

BIBLIOGRAPHY

Elshtain, Jean Bethke and Sheila Tobias, eds. *Women, Militarism, and War.* Savage, Md.: Rowman and Littlefield, 1990.

Enloe, Cynthia. *Bananas, Beaches, and Bases: Making Feminist Sense of International Politics.* Berkeley: University of California Press, 1990.

Enloe, Cynthia. *Does Khaki Become You?* Boston: South End Press, 1983.

Falk, Richard A. "Contending Approaches to World Order." *Journal of International Affairs* 31(2) (Fall/Winter 1977): 171–198.

Falk, Richard A., Samuel S. Kim, and Saul H. Mendolvitz, eds. *Toward a Just World Order.* Boulder: Westview, 1980.

Finn, Geraldine. "Women and the Ideology of Science." *Our Generation* 15(1) (Winter 1982): 40–50.

Flax, Jane. "Postmodernism and Gender Relations in Feminist Theory." *Signs: Journal of Women and Culture in Society* 12(4) (1987): 621–643.

Galtung, Johan. "A Structural Theory of Imperialism." *Journal of Peace Research* 8(2) (1971): 81–117.

Gee, Pauline W. "Ensuring Police Protection for Battered Women: The Scott v. Hart Suit." *Signs: Journal of Women in Culture and Society* 8(3) (Spring 1983): 554–567.

Gerzon, Mark. *A Choice of Heroes: The Changing Face of American Manhood.* Boston: Houghton Mifflin, 1984.

Gill, Stephen and David Law. *The Global Political Economy: Perspectives, Problems, and Policies.* Baltimore: Johns Hopkins Press, 1988.

Gilman, Charlotte Perkins. *Herland.* New York: Pantheon, 1979.

Gilpin, Robert. *The Political Economy of International Relations.* Princeton: Princeton University Press, 1987.

Goetz, Anne Marie. "Feminism and the Limits of the Claim to Know: Contradictions in the Feminist Approach to Women in Development." *Millennium: Journal of International Studies* 17(3) (1988): 477–496.

Grant, Rebecca and Kathleen Newland, eds. *Gender and International Relations.* Bloomington: Indiana University Press, 1991.

Griffin, Susan. *Woman and Nature: The Roaring Inside Her.* New York: Harper & Row, 1978.

Griscom, Joan L. "On Healing the Nature/History Split in Feminist Thought." *Heresies* 4(1) (1981): 4–9.

Haas, Peter M. *Saving the Mediterranean: The Politics of International Environmental Cooperation.* New York: Columbia University Press, 1990.

Hanmer, Jalna and Mary Maynard, eds. *Women, Violence, and Social Control.* Atlantic Highlands, N.J.: Humanities Press International, 1987.

Hansson, Carola and Karin Liden. *Moscow Women.* New York: Pantheon Books, 1983.

Haraway, Donna. *Primate Visions: Gender, Race, and Nature in the World of Modern Science.* New York: Routledge, 1989.

Harding, Sandra. *The Science Question in Feminism.* Ithaca, N.Y.: Cornell University Press, 1986.

BIBLIOGRAPHY

Harding, Sandra and Merrill B. Hintikka, eds. *Discovering Reality*. Dordrecht, Holland: D. Reidel, 1983.

Harris, Adrienne and Ynestra King, eds. *Rocking the Ship of State: Toward a Feminist Peace Politics*. Boulder: Westview, 1989.

Hartsock, Nancy C. M. *Money, Sex, and Power: Toward a Feminist Historical Materialism*. Boston: Northeastern University Press, 1983.

Higonnet, Margaret Randolph, Jane Jenson, Sonya Michel, and Margaret Collins Weitz, eds. *Behind the Lines: Gender and the Two World Wars*. New Haven: Yale University Press, 1987.

Holsti, K. J. *The Dividing Discipline: Hegemony and Diversity in International Theory*. Boston: Allen & Unwin, 1985.

Hunt, Michael H. *Ideology and U.S. Foreign Policy*. New Haven: Yale University Press, 1987.

Independent Commission on Disarmament and Security Issues, *Common Security: A Blueprint for Survival*. New York: Simon and Schuster, 1982.

International Studies Quarterly, Special Issue: Speaking the Language of Exile and Dissidence in International Studies, 34(3) (September 1990).

Isaksson, Eva, ed. *Women and the Military System*. New York: Harvester, Wheatsheaf, 1988.

Jackson, Robert H. and Carl G. Rosberg. "Why Africa's Weak States Persist: The Empirical and the Juridical in Statehood." *World Politics* 35(1) (October 1982): 1–24.

Jaggar, Alison. *Feminist Politics and Human Nature*. Totowa, N.J.: Rowman and Allanheld, 1983.

Jaquette, Jane S. "Women and Modernization Theory: A Decade of Feminist Criticism." *World Politics* 34(2) (January 1982): 267–284.

Kaldor, Mary. "The Global Political Economy." *Alternatives* 11(4) (October 1986): 431–460.

Keller, Evelyn Fox. *A Feeling for the Organism: The Life and Work of Barbara McClintock*. New York: W. H. Freeman, 1983.

Keller, Evelyn Fox. *Reflections on Gender and Science*. New Haven: Yale University Press, 1985.

Keohane, Robert O. *After Hegemony: Cooperation and Discord in the World Political Economy*. Princeton: Princeton University Press, 1984.

Keohane, Robert O., ed., *Neorealism and Its Critics*. New York: Columbia University Press, 1986.

Keohane, Robert O. and Joseph S. Nye. *Power and Interdependence*, 2d ed. Glenview, Ill.: Scott, Foresman, 1989.

King, Ynestra. "Feminism and the Revolt of Nature." *Heresies* 4(1) (1981): 12–16.

Klassen, W., ed. *Dialogue Toward Inter-Faith Understanding*. Tantur/Jerusalem: Ecumenical Institute for Theological Research, 1986.

Kramarae, Cheris and Dale Spender, eds. *The Knowledge Explosion*. Elmsford, N.Y.: Pergamon Press, 1991.

Laclau, Ernesto and Chantal Mouffe. *Hegemony and Socialist Strategy: Towards a Radical Democratic Politics.* London: Vergo, 1985.

Lapid, Yosef. "The Third Debate: On the Prospects of International Theory in a Post-Positivist Era." *International Studies Quarterly* 33(3) (September 1989): 235–254.

Leiss, William. *The Domination of Nature.* New York: George Braziller, 1972.

MacCormack, Carol P. and Marilyn Strathern, eds. *Nature, Culture, and Gender.* Cambridge, England: Cambridge University Press, 1980.

Macdonald, Sharon, Pat Holden, and Shirley Ardener, eds. *Images of Women in Peace and War: Cross-Cultural and Historical Perspectives.* London: Macmillan, 1987.

Machiavelli, Niccolò. *The Prince and the Discourses.* New York: Random House, 1940.

Mathews, Jessica Tuchman. "Redefining Security." *Foreign Affairs* 68(2) (Spring 1989): 162–177.

McClelland, David. *Power: The Inner Experience.* New York: Wiley, 1975.

McGlen, Nancy E. and Meredith Reid Sarkees. "Leadership Styles of Women in Foreign Policy." Unpublished paper, 1990.

McIntosh, Peggy. "Interactive Phases of Curricular Re-Vision: A Feminist Perspective." Wellesley, Mass.: Wellesley College Center for Research on Women, 1983.

Meadows, Donella H., Dennis L. Meadows, Jørgen Randers, and William Behrens III, *The Limits to Growth.* New York: Universe Books, 1972.

Merchant, Carolyn. *Ecological Revolutions: Nature, Gender, and Science in New England.* Chapel Hill: University of North Carolina Press, 1989.

Merchant, Carolyn. *The Death of Nature: Women, Ecology, and the Scientific Revolution.* San Francisco: Harper & Row, 1980.

Mies, Maria. *Patriarchy and Accumulation on a World Scale: Women in the International Division of Labour.* London: Zed Books, 1986.

Millennium: Journal of International Studies, Special Issue: Women and International Relations, 17(3) (Winter 1988).

Mische, Patricia M. "Ecological Security and the Need to Reconceptualize Sovereignty." *Alternatives* 14(4) (October 1989): 389–427.

Molyneux, Maxine. "Mobilization Without Emancipation? Women's Interests, State, and Revolution in Nicaragua." *Feminist Studies* 11(2) (Summer 1985): 227–254.

Moore, Henrietta L. *Feminism and Anthropology.* Minneapolis: University of Minnesota Press, 1988.

Morgenthau, Hans J. *Politics Among Nations: The Struggle for Power and Peace,* 5th ed. New York: Knopf, 1973.

Murphy, Craig and Roger Tooze, eds. *The New International Political Economy.* Boulder: Lynne Rienner, 1991.

Myers, Norman. "Environment and Security." *Foreign Policy* 74 (Spring 1989): 23–41.

Myers, Norman. *Gaia: An Atlas of Planet Management*. New York: Double-day, 1984.

Nathanson, Stephen. "In Defense of Moderate Patriotism." *Ethics* 99 (April 1989): 535–552.

North, Robert C. *War, Peace, Survival: Global Politics and Conceptual Synthesis*. Boulder: Westview, 1990.

Okin, Susan Moller. *Justice, Gender, and the Family*. New York: Basic Books, 1989.

Orr, David W. and Marvin S. Soroos, eds. *The Global Predicament: Ecological Perspectives on World Order*. Chapel Hill: University of North Carolina Press, 1979.

Parker, Geoffrey. *Western Geopolitical Thought in the Twentieth Century*. New York: St. Martin's Press, 1985.

Pateman, Carole. "God Hath Ordained to Man a Helper: Hobbes, Patriarchy, and Conjugal Right." *British Journal of Political Science* 19(4) (October 1989): 445–464.

Pateman, Carole. *The Sexual Contract*. Stanford: Stanford University Press, 1988.

Peterson, V. Spike. "Clarification and Contestation: A Conference Report on 'Women, the State and War': What Difference Does Gender Make?" Los Angeles: Center for International Studies, University of Southern California, 1989.

Peterson, V. Spike, ed. *Gendered States: Feminist (Re)visions of International Relations Theory*. Boulder: Lynne Rienner, 1992.

Phillips, Anne, ed. *Feminism and Equality*. Oxford: Basil Blackwell, 1987.

Pierce, Diana. "The Feminization of Poverty." *Journal for Peace and Justice Studies* 2(1) (1990): 1–20.

Pierson, Ruth Roach, ed. *Women and Peace: Theoretical, Historical, and Practical Perspectives*. London: Croom Helm, 1987.

Pietilä, Hilkka and Jeanne Vickers. *Making Women Matter: The Role of the United Nations*. London: Zed Books, 1990.

Pirages, Dennis. *Global Technopolitics: The International Politics of Technology and Resources*. Belmont, Calif.: Wadsworth, 1989.

Pitkin, Hanna F. *Fortune Is a Woman: Gender and Politics in the Thought of Niccolò Machiavelli*. Berkeley: University of California Press, 1984.

Plant, Judith, ed. *Healing the Wounds: The Promise of Ecofeminism*. Philadelphia: New Society Publishers, 1989.

Pursell, Carroll, ed. *From Conservation to Ecology: The Development of Environmental Concern*. New York: Thomas Crowell, 1973.

Reardon, Betty A. *Sexism and the War System*. New York: Teachers College Press, 1985.

Renner, Michael. *National Security: The Economic and Environmental Dimensions*. Washington, D.C.: Worldwatch Institute, 1989.

Ritvo, Harriet. *The Animal Estate: The English and Other Creatures in the Victorian Age.* Cambridge, Mass.: Harvard University Press, 1987.

Rosaldo, Michelle Z. and Louise Lamphere, eds. *Women, Culture, and Society.* Stanford: Stanford University Press, 1974.

Rosenau, James N., ed. *International Politics and Foreign Policy.* New York: Free Press, 1969.

Rosenberg, Emily S. "Gender." *The Journal of American History* 77(1) (June 1990): 116–124.

Rourke, J. T. *International Politics on the World Stage,* 3d ed. Guilford, Conn.: Dushkin, 1991.

Ruddick, Sara. *Maternal Thinking: Toward a Politics of Peace.* New York: Ballantine Books, 1989.

Runyan, Anne Sisson. "Feminism, Peace, and International Politics: An Examination of Women Organizing Internationally for Peace and Security." Ph.D. diss., American University, 1988.

Runyan, Anne Sisson and V. Spike Peterson. "The Radical Future of Realism: Feminist Subversions of IR Theory." *Alternatives* 16(1) (1991): 67–106.

Schelling, Thomas C. *The Strategy of Conflict.* Cambridge, Mass.: Harvard University Press, 1960.

Scott, Joan W. *Gender and the Politics of History.* New York: Columbia University Press, 1988.

Seager, Joni, ed. *The State of the Earth Atlas.* New York: Simon and Schuster, 1990.

Seager, Joni and Ann Olson. *Women in the World: An International Atlas.* London: Pan Books, 1986.

Segal, Lynne. *Is The Future Female? Troubled Thoughts on Contemporary Feminism.* New York: Peter Bedrick, 1988.

Sen, Amartya. "More Than 100 Million Women Are Missing." *New York Review of Books* 37(20) (1991): 61–66.

Sen, Gita and Caren Grown. *Development, Crises, and Alternative Visions: Third World Women's Perspectives.* New York: Monthly Review Press, 1987.

Shiva, Vandana. "Ecology Movements in India." *Alternatives* 11(2) (April 1986): 255–273.

Shiva, Vandana. *Staying Alive: Women, Ecology, and Development.* London: Zed Books, 1989.

Shiva, Vandana. "The Violence of Reductionist Science." *Alternatives* 12(2) (April 1987): 243–261.

Small, Melvin and J. David Singer. *Resort to Arms: International and Civil Wars, 1816–1980.* Beverly Hills: Sage, 1982.

Snidal, Duncan. "Relative Gains and the Pattern of International Cooperation." *American Political Science Review* 85(3) (1991): 701–726.

Spanier, John. *Games Nations Play*, 6th ed. Washington, D.C.: Congressional Quarterly Press, 1987.

Spender, Dale, ed. *Men's Studies Modified: The Impact of Feminism on the Academic Disciplines*. Oxford: Pergamon Press, 1981.

Sprout, Harold and Margaret Sprout. *The Context of Environmental Politics: Unfinished Business for America's Third Century*. Lexington: The University Press of Kentucky, 1978.

Sprout, Harold and Margaret Sprout. *Toward a Politics of the Planet Earth*. New York: Van Norstrand Reinhold, 1971.

Steuernagel, Gertrude A. and Laurel U. Quinn. "Is Anyone Listening? Political Science and the Response to the Feminist Challenge." Unpublished paper, 1986.

Stiehm, Judith Hicks. *Arms and the Enlisted Woman*. Philadelphia: Temple University Press, 1989.

Stiehm, Judith Hicks. *Women and Men's Wars*. Oxford: Pergamon Press, 1983.

Stiehm, Judith Hicks. *Women's Views of the Political World of Men*. Dobbs Ferry, N.Y.: Transnational Publishers, 1984.

Stockholm International Peace Research Institute (SIPRI). *Policies for Common Security*. London and Philadelphia: Taylor and Francis, 1985.

Sylvester, Christine. "Some Dangers in Merging Feminist and Peace Projects." *Alternatives* 12(4) (October 1987): 493–509.

Tannen, Deborah. *You Just Don't Understand: Women and Men in Conversation*. New York: Morrow, 1990.

Tickner, J. Ann. "Hans Morgenthau's Principles of Political Realism: A Feminist Reformulation." *Millennium* 17(3) (Winter 1988): 429–440.

Tickner, J. Ann. *Self-Reliance Versus Power Politics: The American and Indian Experiences in Building Nation States*. New York: Columbia University Press, 1987.

Tilly, Charles, ed. *The Formation of National States in Western Europe*. Princeton: Princeton University Press, 1975.

Tong, Rosemarie. *Feminist Thought: A Comprehensive Introduction*. Boulder: Westview, 1989.

Ullman, Richard H. "Redefining Security." *International Security* 8(1) (Summer 1983): 129–153.

Vasquez, John, ed. *Classics of International Relations*, 2d ed. Englewood Cliffs, N.J.: Prentice Hall, 1990.

Vickers, Jeanne. *Women and the World Economic Crisis*. London: Zed Books, 1991.

Walker, R. B. J., ed. *Culture, Ideology, and World Order*. Boulder: Westview, 1988.

Wallensteen, Peter, ed. *Peace Research: Achievements and Challenges*. Boulder: Westview, 1988.

Wallerstein, Immanuel. *The Modern World System*. New York: Academic Press, 1974.

Waltz, Kenneth N. *Man, the State, and War*. New York: Columbia University Press, 1959.

Waltz, Kenneth N. *Theory of International Politics*. Boston: Addison-Wesley, 1979.

Waring, Marilyn. *If Women Counted: A New Feminist Economics*. San Francisco: Harper & Row, 1988.

White, Lynn. "The Historical Roots of Our Ecological Crisis." *Science*, March 10, 1987.

Williams, Michael C. "Rousseau, Realism, and *Realpolitik*." *Millennium: Journal of International Studies* 18(2): 185–203.

Wilson, G. Kenneth and Peter Wallensteen. *Major Armed Conflicts in 1987*. Uppsala, Sweden: Department of Peace and Conflict Research, Uppsala University, 1988.

World Commission on Environment and Development. *Our Common Future*. Oxford: Oxford University Press, 1987.

Index

Galbraith, J. K., 67
Games, 83, 156n28
Gandhi, Indira, 125
Gee, Pauline, 57
Gender definitions, 7–8
Geopolitics, 24, 100–101, 109–11, 112–13
Germany, 68
Gerzon, Mark, 139
Gilman, Charlotte Perkins, 59
Gilpin, Robert, 69
Global modeling, 113
Goetz, Anne Marie, 95
"The Golden Ass" (Machiavelli), 47
Great powers: environmental degradation by, 118; in international relations theory, 18; in post-Cold War period, 19–20; realist study of, 10, 12, 29; *see also* Soviet-American relations
Great Wall of China, 112
Greeks, ancient, 37–38, 40, 82, 149n18
Green Belt Movement, 125
Greenham Common demonstration, 60
Green Revolution, 121
Griscom, Joan, 124
Group of Seven, 148n2

Haiti, 115
Haraway, Donna, 148–49n13
Harding, Sandra, 64–65, 72–73, 103–4, 120
Hare, Nathan, 116
Hartsock, Nancy, 72, 73–74
Harvard Negotiation Project, 139
Hegemonic masculinity: alternatives to, 139; defined, 6; ecofeminism and, 98; global security and, 129–30; international relations theories and, 131; Marxist analysis and, 86; "political man" and, 37; "rational economic man"

and, 72; realist assumptions and, 30, 36, 62; of Thatcher, 146n6; warrior-citizenship and, 38, 58
Herland (Gilman), 59
Herz, John, 148n5
Hierarchical dualisms, 8, 126
Hiroshima, 151n61
Hobbes, Thomas, 28, 45–46, 110–11, 151n51
Hofstede, Geert, 140, 141, 160n8
"Home" concept, 81
Homosexuality, 6
"Housewifization," 81, 87–88
Hunt, Michael, 49
Hussein, Saddam, 41–42, 150n32

Identity, national, 137–38
Imperialism, *see* Colonialism
Independent Commission on Disarmament and Security Issues, 52, 53
Indian women, 57, 88–89
Industrial Revolution, 81
Infanticide, 89
Instrumental rationality, 73, 78
Interdependence: in African worldview, 65; autonomy and, 32, 64; cooperation and, 63, 74, 133; economic, 12, 79; international relations theory and, 20
International Congress of Women (1915), 54
International Labor Office, 75
International Monetary Fund, 78, 93
Is the Future Female? (Segal), 136

Jackson, C. D., 49–50
Jaggar, Alison, 74
Jain, Devaki, 67, 155n14
Japan, 68
Jaquette, Jane, 65
Job opportunities, 56, 86
Journal articles, 146n11

3/00²